"This book will bring you back in tune with
and why you're here in the first place. Reading *Language of the Feminine*
brought me to a place of purpose, awareness and understanding; it was
like taking a deep breath".
—Toni Bate, Creative Director, INDIE PUBLISHING LIMITED, Scotland, UK.

"I love this book about feeling fully alive as a woman! In my work with
women, I see how they desire to be more in tune with something. Often
they do not exactly know with what, but they do know, it is something
other than goals, stress, to-do lists or to-be lists...

Jane offers such a rich palette for women. She invites us to open
ourselves on a daily basis for so many different things that surround us by
nature. It is an eye-opener on how little we need to be able to recalibrate
ourselves. She opens many doors and offers clear steps to help women
find their own style, inner wisdom and inner guidance. She widens our
perception on the variety of ways available to us, to find our own unique
inner mentor. This is how we tune-in to receive infinite support. Thank you
Jane!"
—Marijke Derèse, Psychotherapist, WOMEN'S WORK AT ESSENSUAL, Belgium.

"Jane Cormack skilfully brings a full and deep understanding, through her
passion and study of the feminine and creativity, in her book, *Language
of the Feminine*. This is a universal language we all, women and men,
can draw upon. It's our innate, intuitive nature, but often needs to be
fully recognised and reenergised. At the end of each chapter, Jane offers
exercises and journaling, through questioning and personal examples; it
helps us explore and harness this language—to be our full potential—the
echo of our own heart".
—Joan Greenblatt, cofounder of the INNER DIRECTIONS FOUNDATION, author
of Healing with Flower Essences, San Diego, California.

"At a moment in time, when the world is calling us all to reconnect to the Deep Feminine within, comes this wonderful guide, *Language of the Feminine*, to help reconnect us to our true feminine power. Many women are lost in understanding what, 'the deep feminine' really means; they do not know, in this fast moving, materialistic-oriented world, how to find their own purpose, beauty and self-love. The common attitudes of our current culture, are about 'comparison' and 'more' and 'now'. The impact of this 'not knowing' on our society is tremendous. Jane Cormack guides us to understand where our true roots are by using self-inquiry projects to reach a more trusting, complete and truer aspect of Self. This is a beautiful book for all young women, women young at heart, and women encouraged to find themselves and their true power, at whatever stage of life".
—Sabina Rademacher, Coach & Facilitator in Leadership, Finding your True Purpose and Sacred Intimacy and RISING WOMEN RISING WORLD, Berlin.

"I loved this book, a lot! Every time I sat down to read it, I felt at peace. The language is so poetic and sophisticated and the whole cultural and artistic heritage of Jane is palpable. I felt the energy behind every word in total alignment with who she is and the work she is doing in the world. The language, topics and whole spirit of the book is so feminine and felt soothing to my soul. For a modern women—who is too often living from her masculine essence— just reading this book would be therapy to bring her energies into balance".
—Nora Nagy, Health & Beauty Coach, HERE & NOW, Berlin.

"Jane so beautifully, and in depth, describes the many varieties of the Language of the World, all of those voices that I already listen to, so reading this book was confirmation that I'm doing something right! And the real, personal stories make it so fresh to read. If you want to learn how you can listen to and trust your own intuition more accurately, and how to read the signs sent to us from the universe, guiding us through our lives all the time, this is a great book for you".
—Kamila Plihalova, Founder of INSPIRE BY CHOICE, Czech Republic.

Language
of the
Feminine

Awaken the Source of Your Creative,
Intuitive & Sensual Self

Language
of the
Feminine

Awaken the Source of Your Creative, Intuitive & Sensual Self

Jane A. Cormack

SOURCE
PUBLISHING

www.JaneCormack.com

Source Publishing™
www.LanguageoftheFeminine.com

Published by Source Publishing

ISBN: 978-1-5262-0524-7

Cover & book design by CenterPointe Media
www.CenterPointeMedia.com

Dedication

For the beauty, bounty, fertile and
creative source of our Mother Earth,
the place we all call *home*.

Contents

Introduction

Part One

CHAPTER ONE
Learning the Language of the World

CHAPTER TWO
The Forgotten Language of Pleasure

Part Two

CHAPTER THREE
The Language of Your Body

CHAPTER FOUR

The Language of Feminine Power

CHAPTER FIVE

The Language of Love and Relationships

CHAPTER SIX
The Language of Giving and Receiving

CHAPTER SEVEN
The Language of Home and Sanctuary

Part Three

CHAPTER ELEVEN
The Language of Word and Symbols

Part Four

CHAPTER TWELVE
The Language of Purpose

CHAPTER THIRTEEN
The Language of Freedom

Contents

Introduction

*I*n 1973, Anthony Hopkins accepted the starring role in George Feifer's, The Girl from Petrovka, based on the book by the same name. Wanting to read the book for research, he searched many bookstores in London but could not find a copy.

Giving up and going home, he spied an abandoned book sitting on a bench—a copy of The Girl from Petrovka.

Two years later during filming, George Feifer admitted to Hopkins that he didn't even have a copy of his own book, because a friend he loaned it to in London had lost it, "Complete with all of my annotations", said Feifer. Hopkins pulled out his copy. "This one?" he asked.

It was the same book.

There are many 'lenses' through which we can view life. Our family, social, cultural and religious upbringings give us certain lenses to look through that can magnify or distort our vision. Through the content and journey of this book, I offer life through what may be a new kind of lens to you. It is a lens that focuses on connections that are often overlooked, yet have always existed and reveals a language symbiotically woven through all living and non-living things on this planet, including us. It comprises the language of everything; it is the Language of the World.

In revealing our connection with this language, we also expose an intrinsic connection to life, to our planet and to each other. We enter into a multi-way conversation that never ends and discover new ways of communicating with the universe, ourselves and one another that can guide us to be present, in the deepest experience of each moment.

The golden threads that weave through this book are the Language of the Feminine and the Goddess of Pleasure. Elements that need their resurrection in all areas of life. You may well wonder what the Language of the World has got to do with the feminine, with pleasure or music, sound or nature, freedom, purpose or home and sanctuary. All of these things may not appear connected, but they are.

This book brings these connections together through both the physical components of life and with our divine nature, helping you navigate a path to a place of understanding your feminine wholeness. The Language of the Feminine can be a portal through which we realise our interconnectedness with all of life by awakening the source of our intuition, our feminine essence, pleasures, creative life-force and natural sensual nature. This book, in and of itself, is an expression of the Language of the Feminine; flowing, organic in its movement with powerful peaks, primal, grounded and connected to Earth, revealing her love, softness and vulnerability with pockets of playfulness, sensuality and alive with creativity.

As a society, we have come to value the more linear and structured ways of life, which represent the masculine element. Yet, by allowing this element to rule our lives, we miss a vital part of ourselves. Our feminine element is acutely under-recognised and is the missing language that affects all of our relationships; how we treat ourselves, one another and the planet.

During the journey of this book, we explore this feminine language in a very tactile way through the relationships we have with our own bodies, with people and our homes, our creative expressions and purpose; with the natural world and the divine element that flows through it all. These relationships form the unique way in which we each interact with life and the universe. Through understanding these relationships, we create strong foundations in earth and body, and to the divine source that exists within every element of life. Your very own unique language is revealed.

There is great mystery in our universe and so much that we don't know. And, I don't believe we need to or can 'know it all'. To do so would render a pointless journey while we are on the planet. Part of the joy of life is its slow unravelling—the mysterious connections and magical links that we see over time if we can trust in the 'knowing' that all we do need to know will be revealed in the moment that we need it.

Imagine dissecting a beautiful lilac flower, an iris. We pluck out and unravel its inner core, pull all the petals off and then peel all the fibres from the stem, one by one, to figure out how it was put together. But we can never put it back together in the same way; its wholeness has been tampered with. Our minds may be satiated knowing its design, but in breaking it, a part of its great beauty and essence has been destroyed. We destroy the very thing that ignited our curiosity in the first place. In dissecting, we often squeeze out the joy.

We can still explore, deepen our connections, our knowledge and grow; we can still place this flower under a microscope and look closely at its beauty and design while it remains whole. This takes trust in the knowledge that everything is as it should be and trust in the unfolding of our lives and the universe.

Imagine if we knew everything there was to know—what's around every corner and how our daily lives would play out; God we'd be bored!

NAVIGATING THE UNIVERSAL MAP—THIS BOOK

What I share in this book is the sum of many of my own life experiences, visions, intuition, inner knowing and learning from the many messengers on my path. You've picked it up for good reason. Trust that. It is the Language of the World speaking with you.

This book has been written over a period of time and has been formed through an organic, feminine process. It has been a journey in which I have not tried to 'uniform' my voice because that would not reflect who I am and the way that women are. We have many voices and aspects to our nature that we often try to constrict, hold in, hold back, hide or fit into clearly labelled categories.

It's primarily a book for women, but men are also welcome, as we all hold both masculine and feminine elements within; it is a guide to embodying our 'feminine wholeness' through re-discovering forgotten pleasures, *listening* to our natural intuitive abilities and developing clear confidence in the unique ways we each perceive life. This book may also act as a catalyst, awakening seeds of ancient feminine wisdom that you already hold within and thus, you may be reminded of what you already know. These seeds of ancient wisdom are scattered throughout this book in which I share many of my own personal experiences of listening and communicating with the Language of the World as 'how to' examples. My hope is that this book will help you trust yourself deeply, understand and embrace your true essence, while giving you simple, practical tools and exercises to learn and enjoy.

I offer some reading tips to enhance your experience >

- Pay close attention to how you feel while you read the book.
- It's a book to feel, not to judiciously over-analyse, you'll get the most from it reading this way.
- Take what resonates, leave what doesn't, maybe for later.
- You can read the entire book from start to finish to get the big picture and to hear the resounding Language of the World OR you can use the book like an oracle, opening it randomly to receive some guidance or a message.

- I use a certain language in this book that could be deemed 'spiritual', which may be familiar to you, but if not, please read chapter one first; 'Learning the Language of the World' in which I outline my definition of languages as well as the phrase 'Language of the World'.

- Source: In this book I use the term 'source' to reference what I understand to be what others may call God, divinity or life-force energy. It is the source of all that is. It is a higher power imbued within all of life, it is the universe and it is you and I. It is the timeless, divine place within our own being; it is the essence and the core, the foundations and the origins. In referring to source, I also focus on two places or 'homes' where source 'is'. The first home is within each and every human being and living thing. The second home of source exists within and out of this world, it is everywhere and everything. It is the vast, unknowable, unfathomable pulse of the universe.

- Dive in and enjoy with an open heart and mind; what you take from this book may be more, less or otherwise than you expect.

Part One

CHAPTER ONE

Learning the Language
of the World

The world or universe will use any means by which to communicate with us; smell, sound, thought, word, music, object, media, visions, dreams, colours, nature, books, internet, people, animals, numbers; the list goes on. The universe is communicating with you right now because you are reading this book. We are in constant communication with our surroundings and although the language is always there, we don't always listen. When we learn to pay attention and develop awareness of this language, when the whispers from the universe become real conversations, we are guided to the very best of what is possible for us each day.

The Language of the World encompasses a universal form of communication in which we receive and can *be* the guidance; whether that guidance comes from inside or outside of us. I believe you already listen to this language, often in ways that you may not be consciously aware of or have even imagined. This book will help guide you to learn how to become more conscious of this language *and* why it's also often a good thing to switch off mentally and trust your body to 'be' the language.

The Language of the World can leave us speechless and utterly in awe of how magical life can actually be. Do not underestimate the quality that magic, mystery and pleasure bring to our lives. The earlier story of Hopkins and the journey of his book demonstrates that life is incredibly magical and interconnected; it is a mirror that reflects both ways. The less we see ourselves as separate from the universe and everything in this intricate energetic web, the more we can flow in the co-creative elements of our inner and outer world.

I first read *The Alchemist* by Paulo Coelho around the age of twenty. Coelho uses the term 'Language of the World' in his book to reference how we communicate with the world and how the world also 'speaks' to us. A few years later, a specific moment made me very aware of how this language works and I began to notice this everyday language in the world around me. I forgot about the book and came to believe I had coined the phrase 'Language of the World' myself, right up until the near completion of this book. So in writing about the Language of the World, I honour the influence of Paulo Coelho and his book, *The Alchemist*. Yet I write from my own embodied experience of what the Language of the World is over many years, since the seed was first planted in my mind and heart.

THE LANGUAGE OF EVERYTHING

Everything has a language that is born of the essence of what it is. Objects such as lamp shades or teapots have a visual language expressed through their appearance; their shape, material, colour, pattern, texture and size. They also have a practical purpose and a sound, like the chink of placing the ceramic lid on a teapot. Designers know how to express a certain language in the way that they arrange a space with colour, objects and light. They can create an ambience that speaks to our emotions, so that when we walk into their room, it influences how we feel. A piece of jewellery also has a language; it can feel bold and strong or ethereal and light. Its language is expressed through its form, size, colour, the materials used and the inspiration and energy of the person who designed and made the piece. Plants, people, animals, books, computers, you name it; they all express a visual language of what they are.

So let's make a differentiation here; the Language of the World is multi-layered, but we will focus on two layers:

1. The way that the Universe communicates through the sensory (visual, audio, taste, touch) language of 'objects'.
2. The way that humans communicate and converse with everything in, on and around this planet through the energy of consciousness.

So let's look at the first layer using an 'object' such as a turquoise ceramic teapot as an example. A teapot is an object that has a visual language; it has its own essence or 'total', which is the sum of all its parts. Its parts can comprise of shape, colour, texture, design, usefulness and the energy of the designer and maker. The universe has its own intelligence and plays an active part in co-creatively speaking to us via objects. The conversation begins when we come into contact with the presence of an object, like the teapot. When certain objects are brought into our awareness they seem to 'pop out' from the ordinary background of life. And, because we all have individual associations and memories attached to objects, the language of this object activates an emotional, mental, physical or energetic response within us, just as a sound or scent might. The teapot then becomes more than the total sum of its parts. The Language of the World uses sounds, scents, objects and more, to focus and direct our attention and to guide us. Thus, the language of everything becomes the Language of the World.

On the second layer, the Language of the World is the language understood by nature, by animals and by our own deeper or higher awareness.

This language pertains to the Language of the Feminine as it encompasses the intuitive and often subtle sensations associated with our feminine element. When we awaken to this language, we can clearly communicate with the entire natural world, including the 'soul' of this planet. It is a soul to soul language through which we can sense messages in the movement of the wind, with animals and plants—and begin to understand the Earths rhythms and how they apply to our own life rhythms. We are all born with this natural ability that sometimes simply needs to be re-activated to remember primal seeds of knowledge that we already have within.

Since this language can often be very subtle, many of us follow it without conscious awareness. It can be a moment when your body acts as a compass, leading you naturally, without thought to a magical moment, a nice connection, a small joy within your day or a challenging opportunity to stretch yourself further. The Language of the World can lead us to these moments all of the time.

It's a misconception to think that listening to and following the guidance of the Language of the World always leads us to some big, lightening-striking, life changing moment. Yes, that does of course happen, yet the Language of the World and its often subtle guidance wants us to see, be in and experience the immense joy and beauty available to us in as many moments as possible.

The multitude of daily magical moments available to us can revive our sense of wonder and excitement for life and deepen our feelings of joy. These simple, uplifting moments speak to our hearts and remind us why we are alive. They lift us from our perpetual, repetitive thought processes and bring us back to our own sense of self, presence and peace.

These small moments in time may arrive during a hike in nature, when you are just walking where your body leads you to go:

Imagine that you have arrived by a riverside. There's something magical in the air, in the way that the sunlight is shining through the trees, highlighting the soft, green moss so exquisitely. You're there just in time to witness a wild otter playing and swimming in the river. As you watch the otter, you see and feel how free it is and how much pleasure it takes play-ing in the river. You feel uplifted and honoured to witness and connect with this wild animal when you are alone. It's as if that moment were designed especially for you. You are reminded of what pleasure and freedom feel like and decide that you want more of it in your life. (This happened to me last week!).

The Language of the World has spoken. It has ignited a memory within you that you may have forgotten. Experiencing pleasurable, yet simple moments such as this one, make every day special.

The experience of feeling intuitively drawn to such moments can act like a map. Your guidance and the way that you receive it is your inner compass and everything in the universe is your map, including you. But how do you use such a map? This language and map is as ever changing as you are. It can guide you to moments of joy in your day or to a person who impacts you to the degree that you completely change your life and direction. This map can guide you to a deeply desired intimate relation-ship, to an opportunity to share your art, an invitation to a nature hike and picnic, to speak to a large audience about your work or to a moment that stretches you beyond your comfort zone. The Language of the World has provided you with an infinite map that you are co-creating. If you follow it, if you listen, moment to moment, it will lead you to what you wish to experience and where you desire to be.

TRUST

Our mainstream culture programs us not to trust ourselves and continu-ously plants seeds of doubt via our media, education systems, social or religious conditions, which can inhibit our ability to believe and explore more expansive possibilities and potentials. We are not taught to be innovators, to do things differently, to understand our emotions or how to navigate relationships in these systems. We are not taught to trust the instinctive, wild ideas that emerge within our being, to follow the flow of energy without knowing why, to be led by the pounding impulse to move, to go, to begin. "That's just crazy, why would you do that? What's the point of going there? I'm not sure if that's a good idea". Thus, seeds of doubt are planted; the unconscious questioning of others is often a test of our own sense of trust in ourselves. Without your trust, you will not listen and follow.

Trusting can be scary. It often means saying 'yes' when you don't know how you will do, say or be what you are guided to. A leap into the unknown is based entirely upon your faith. It is self-trust. You can't possibly know what the results will be. All you have is a feeling that it's a good choice to make in that moment. Maybe it's an excited feeling, light and joyful, it may feel expansive within your body or you may feel some kind of release of tension and excited nervousness or contentment when you make a decision.

Risk is involved in making decisions because we don't really know what the outcome will be. Even 'planned' choices that we think should result in solid outcomes often do not work out exactly in the way we planned. Sometimes the outcome is much better than we ever could have anticipated. It is the organic nature of life and growth, which is why we need to leave some spaciousness within the plans for the journey and results to exceed our limited expectations. If you look at life from this perspective, then *every* decision you make is risky. Deciding to go to the local cafe for a morning coffee could be considered risky because although the 'plan' is to go to the cafe and order a coffee, there are a million other unknown factors that could happen. You may bump into an old friend on the way and invite them to join you. You might get half-way there and realise you left your wallet at home and go back to get it. The cafe might have run out of coffee so you might have to drink tea instead. What a disaster!

Sometimes we need to make a move or a decision when we can't access the 'knowing' within, but we know we need to create movement so *something* needs to be chosen. Often after making such choices, we can feel like it wasn't the 'right' move to make. Yet in hindsight, we usually find that it's only by taking the first step and making the choice, that we discover what it feels like and if it is indeed what we wanted. We are always free to choose again and again. Without trusting ourselves and our ability to make choices, we never really experience the full abundance, depth and richness of the human experience. Trust evolves as we take each step, trusting that we will know what the next step to take will be when we get there.

It can take immense trust and courage to listen to yourself and follow the guidance that appears from the Language of the World, because often it will not lead you to where you expect it to. Sometimes you may not even know why your guidance leads you in a certain direction. But the mind asks you 'why' and wants to have a damn good reason for taking such risks. Listen to your mind's questioning, it wants to keep you safe. But if your linear, logical thinking is too controlled and tight and you continue to trust your mind over your heart and internal guidance, you continue a life of safety and stifle truly living the life you want. A full, alive life involves the integration of our logic and intellect, our timeless internal wisdom and following guidance; it involves our wholeness, which mirrors the integration and dance between the masculine and feminine elements within us. Life is constantly asking us to open and trust again, even after our trust has been broken so many times.

LANGUAGE AND COMMUNICATION

There are around 7,097 known living languages in the world today and the number of people speaking these languages ranges from 1,197 million to just one or two. Of those languages 1,531 (22%) are in danger of extinction and 916 (13%) of known languages are on their way to being extinct. This means that only 50 people or less still actively use the language or that *"Only a few elderly speakers are still living"*.[1] A total of 367 languages have become extinct since 1950 at a rate of approximately six per year. Within a century, it's likely that the number of living languages will be cut at least in half and may be even fewer than 1,000. Much of the reason for this, is that new generations are not being taught these ancient languages because it's unnecessary for them to learn them as the world becomes more of a global community. The most commonly spoken languages in the world, with more than 100 million native speakers are Mandarin, Spanish and English and the number of people speaking these languages will certainly expand in the coming years.

This data shows that the way people communicate through language is constantly changing. Technology is making the world smaller by the minute through our ability to communicate and connect with a global population, and so a common language, such as English, is often used. Everything evolves which results in the dying out of what may not serve us anymore. Even so, some people may feel a loss of cultural identity or tradition.

When we think of language, we usually think of linguistics, yet language is a general term for communication that encompasses the multiple ways that we give and receive information or knowledge. In 2004/2005, I lived in Australia and shared an apartment for a while with a woman

---

[1] Quote Source: http://www.ethnologue.com/endangered-languages. All figures were correct at the time of publishing.

named Pam. She worked as a sign language interpreter within the deaf community. Pam shared with me the documentary, *In a Small Valley (Deafness in Australia)*[2], which focuses on the story of Peter Adams, an intelligent and articulate artist who has been profoundly deaf from the age of two. As well as following the story of Peter's life, several interviews with other deaf people were included. I was utterly fascinated by how a deaf person's visual world can be more acute than a hearing person's world and that the sensory world of blind people becomes highly evolved when one sense is impaired. The various ways that people learn to communicate are extraordinary.

Auslan, a shorthand, almost hieroglyphic way of signing was developed in the late 1970s and early 1980s. This is a visual language that is rhythmical, fast and theatrical in its often large or dramatic movements. Like actors and actresses, through Auslan, the deaf community learned to visually act and amplify their physicality to express themselves. They developed many different languages which could be expressed through the body, as well as through touch and feeling the vibration of vocal chords.

OUR PERCEIVED LANGUAGE BARRIERS

In as much as all forms of language are imbued with unique sounds, fluctuations, vibrations, visual movement, music, beauty, poetry and wisdom; language can also create perceived barriers to clear and authentic communication. You may have experienced travelling in foreign countries where you couldn't understand the language. Maybe you found it frustrating at times, desperately wanting to know what the man at the market said to you or maybe you had fun for a while using a jumble of words, sign

---

[2] * In *a Small Valley (Deafness in Australia)*, Dir. Dennis K. Smith, Producer, Jack White, (Melbourne, Australia, 1996, Open Channel Productions).

language and pointing at things. And perhaps, with certain people, there was an unspoken 'knowing' where words even felt unnecessary.

Human's have developed so many different ways to communicate and often express similar sentiments in diverse ways, an example of which we can see most clearly within the common threads or 'truths' of our world's religions. When we learn to 'see through' the linguistic language of expression and widen our perception of what language is, we can find hidden connections that we were not aware of simply because linguistics got in the way.

LEARNING A NEW LANGUAGE

Whilst on a train journey from Forres to Aberdeen in Scotland, a robust, bearded man with circular spectacles got on the train and sat down opposite me. He immediately answered a call on his mobile phone and began speaking Gaelic. Gaelic is one of the ancient, native languages of Scotland and sounds similar to Scandinavian languages to me. Although I'm Scottish, it took me a moment to realise that this bearded man was speaking Gaelic, because I don't speak it. After his call, we began chatting about language, he shared with me that he was a Gaelic language teacher and had recently returned from Hawaii where he had been studying the Hawaiian language. I told him that I'd also recently returned from Hawaii and loved the musicality of their language. It turned out that he wasn't just any language teacher; he taught adults how to learn a language the easy way—through action and doing rather than reading and writing. He told me that adults learn languages 57% faster than children do.

This surprised me as I always thought it was easier to learn anything as a child. What the bearded man told me during our train journey was that because adults have gathered so many more skills than children, basically by having lived longer and done more, that it's easier to learn by action because there is so much more to reference. Learning by action means using physical and practical ways to teach that incorporate movement and life experiences, rather than only learning through mind-based tools like reading and writing. Using purely mind-based tools to learn anything new takes us much longer.

Like learning any new language, the Language of the World can take time to integrate into your awareness. But the great thing about this language is that you're not starting from scratch. The Language of the World works in unison with the language of your whole being. It means, in different moments, to follow your heart, follow your bliss; to follow what feels good. Choosing this path does not mean that you will avoid challenges. That's impossible. Life is filled with challenges that allow us to grow and learn. Joy can still be present during these challenges, when we follow our hearts and the guidance that shows up along the way.

There are a number of ways to learn a new language. When it comes to learning the Language of the World, we tune-in to this language through our feelings. The Language of the World can still speak to us through the words we see, read or hear, but it's the *feeling* elicited by seeing, reading or hearing those words that I'll show you how to pay more attention to.

The possibilities of what can unfold when we truly listen to the Language of the World can be profound:

In 2012, I went on a tour around Scotland with a friend while video blogging and writing my personal experiences for this book. In-between my friend leaving and my partner arriving, I had a few days on my own, in a lodge on the Isle of Mull in the Inner Hebrides. I spent the interim time writing more content for this book.

One day, while standing at the front of the lodge for a tea break, I began chatting with a blonde English girl who was temporarily in charge of the lodge; she was having a cigarette break. She soon began to tell me her story about how she had recently quit her job in construction engineering, sold her house and split up with her boyfriend. She began the conversation by telling me how, at the time of her decisions, she was aware of the signs of the universe that were guiding her to change her course of action; "It's kind of like the 'Language of the World'", she said. I told her excitedly, that I was writing a book with that title, at that very moment, upstairs in the lodge! She then told me that she began reading a book on this subject several times, but never finished it; it was the world-famous, bestselling book, The Alchemist, by Paulo Coelho, which I had read many years before. I recommended that she try to finish it as it's such a simple, yet profound story. She agreed that she'd try to find a copy and see if she could read it to the end this time.

On that note, she told me about the movie, The Butterfly Effect[3], starring Ashton Kutcher, which focuses on the idea that even the smallest choices we make each day can drastically alter the course and direction of our lives. I'd heard of the movie before but had never watched it. After chatting a while longer, it was time for both of us to get back to work

---

[3] The Butterfly Effect. Dir. Eric Bress, J. MacKye Gruber. (USA, 2004, New Line Cinema).

and so I went upstairs to continue writing this book. I sat down at my desk and began shuffling the stuff on it to create some space. Earlier in the day, I had chosen two DVD's from the library in the lounge as potential watching material for later that evening. One was Monty Python and the Holy Grail and the other a period drama which I can't remember the name of. I opened the box of one DVD and inside, instead of the Holy Grail, there was a copy of The Butterfly Effect. To me, this turned out to be like finding the Holy Grail! My jaw dropped. Quite clearly, the Language of the World was talking to me. I listened and later that evening watched the movie. It created quite an impact in my thinking at that time. Its message for me was to be fully conscious of the choices I was making in my life, because each small choice could, quite radically, change my reality and my direction. Our individual choices also create a ripple, affecting other people and their lives. Our choices affect 'the whole' because we are all an intrinsic part of the 'wholeness' of life and the universe. The concept of the movie also appeared in my dreams that night as I experienced the results of making a variety of choices in my current situation through conscious dreaming.

But it doesn't end there; the following day I saw the girl again and she told me that the previous night, she had been clearing the lounge in the lodge. Whilst removing the cushions on the sofa to clean behind them, she discovered a plastic bag. When she opened it, she found one item inside; it was a copy of The Alchemist. She excitedly shared her story with me thinking what a coincidence it was given our conversation the previous day. When I told her how I had found The Butterfly Effect instead of the Holy Grail, she almost fell over. She *enthusiastically proceeded to tell everybody who was staying in the lodge what had happened.*

The synchronicity of becoming involved in that conversation whilst writing this book *and* finding the movie and book referencing the Language of the World is a clear example of how the Language of the World speaks to us. I watched the movie and received a message for myself that was a catalyst for me to be more conscious of my choices. I don't know whether the girl ever finished reading *The Alchemist* or not; we always have a choice whether to listen to the Language of the World and receive its guidance or to carry on as usual. But, when we do listen, we receive the rewards of abundance, guidance and wisdom we were searching for.[4]

Pleasure is one of the feelings that strongly guides us forward, such as my desire to watch a movie in the previous story. It's kind of like the path of least resistance, observing where the doors are opening rather than trying to break down the closed ones. In the following chapter, we explore the language of pleasure.

---

[4] To watch the video in which I share this story on the Isle of Mull, go here: http://www.janecormack.com/rhythmic-inspiration-news/how-to-be-inspired-even-when-you-feel-flat-on-tour-from-mull-in-scotland/.

Chapter Summary

- Everything has a language
  1. The language of 'things'
  2. The language of soul or consciousness
- Learn to trust yourself, your intuition and ideas no matter how wild they may seem
- We communicate in multiple ways all of the time which include visually, vibrationally and energetically as well as through linguistics
- You already know how to speak the Language of the World and have a foundation to build from because it unconsciously happens anyway

CHAPTER TWO

The Forgotten Language
of Pleasure

Pleasure plumps us up, full and vivacious, joyful and juicy; we are the grapes heavy on the vine of life. Ripe and pulsating, ready to burst with sweet delight, we share the overflow. Life vines left unfed, shrivelled and gnarled, dry, withering bodies and souls gasping for sustenance, for just a drop of the divine wine to enliven the senses. Pleasures forgotten, raisins scatter the ground.

I say, 'forgotten', because pleasure is underrated, ignored, experienced in tiny increments and for so many stressed out women, has more or less been squeezed out of the human experience. For many people, pleasure is contained to very specific moments and a limited range of experiences. Containment *is* a part of the pleasure experience, of satiation and reaching 'fullness', but pleasure can be brought into many areas of our daily lives. Let's spread the pleasure word so that more moments of our days are plumped up with pleasure, rather than dried out with dread.

The notion of 'pleasurable' experiences is often connected to some kind of material consumerism or sexuality. Advertising plays on how much better, sexier, attractive or youthful we'll feel after buying the new thing; be that satiny lingerie, the latest iPhone or kitchen gadget.

We can certainly enjoy and experience a very healthy surface kind of pleasure in these things that delight us; satiny lingerie can make us feel a little more sensual and playful and kitchen gadgets can make life easier. But the kind of pleasure I talk about moves far deeper under the surface. This kind of pleasure melts the body, it delights the senses, and it surrenders us to a state of bliss and deep satisfaction. In that state, we are *allowing* the unfolding and unwrapping of something exquisite, delicious and divine. Pleasure is healing for our body, mind and spirit. It is an expression of love and kindness that we can give to ourselves and others. When we acknowledge what gives us pleasure and allow ourselves to experience it, all spheres of life are influenced and 'filled' with more joy and abundance.

JOY AND PLEASURE

Joy and pleasure are similar, yet they elicit different feeling states in the body. In my experience, joy feels uplifting, exciting, elevated, light and expansive and is often felt through the heart. Whereas pleasure feels deep, velvety, relaxing, surrendered, releasing and can be experienced within and throughout the whole body. **It is a whole body experience.**

Life is *meant* to be both joyful and pleasurable. Pleasure can be experienced in every area of life and we can even experience joy in our most challenging moments. Through the release of sadness or loss, we allow ourselves to experience and acknowledge our deepest emotions and our entire emotional spectrum; in these moments, we can feel incredibly alive and connected to all of life.

Pleasure is intrinsically linked to both giving and receiving,[5] yet to receive, we must allow ourselves to do so. We have to learn how to be open or 'receptive' enough to let in the pleasure. If a door is closed and locked, we cannot walk through it or allow what wants to come in to be received. If we feel closed to receiving and experiencing pleasure, then life can feel

[5] More on Giving and Receiving in chapter 6.

skeletal, dull and flat, rather than full, vibrant and alive.

But even if the door is a little ajar, there is an invitation to enter and to open the door further. In opening the door just a little, we open ourselves to receive more pleasure as well as potential pain; we let more of everything available in and in doing so, have a richer and fuller experience of life. It is a choice as to what you wish to let in while both respecting how far you are able to open at this point and where your resistance to opening is holding you back.

Listening to the Language of the World *and* our pleasure pointers can lead us anywhere to do anything. These are the experiences and things that make our souls happy that we might never have imagined could and also sometimes that we did. We may not be doing anything in particular at all and yet we feel a profound sense of pleasure and joy.

Humans are conditioned to look at what needs healing—what is wrong that needs to be righted—what is broken that needs to be fixed and what is lacking. Pleasure is usually a second thought, if it is indeed a thought at all, after the fixing and healing have happened. Healing is deep work, yet joy, pleasure and play are deeply healing.

Where your attention goes, your energy flows. In other words, whatever you focus your attention on gets amplified and grows. It is the nature of energy and why our thoughts and feelings contain such power. My first yoga teacher told me this when I was eighteen and suffering immensely from a severe blushing problem. When a lot of attention and energy was placed on me, I started to go red. And because I was focusing on my rosy face, it made the experience ten times worse. I was more embarrassed that my discomfort was so visible than actually *feeling* embarrassed about anything. I missed so many opportunities to connect with other people. I avoided certain social situations and devised clever strategies that would divert attention away from me.

'Healing', whatever we might consider that to be, automatically happens when we begin to place our attention where we really want it to be. That's not to say that we should ignore the darker aspects of our nature. Our dark aspects are not in need of 'fixing', but require us to embrace and see them, as we do our 'acceptable', light aspects; they create the wholeness of who we are, but are often suppressed within. Yet, we can still reach the place of wholeness that we seek when we focus on what lights us up, because in focusing on this desire, there is *less* room for feelings of lack and unworthiness to enter. Healing can feel complex as we begin to untangle and uncover our true emotions. I see healing as a dance, during which our mind and instincts can merge. We do not need to continually focus on the dance steps that keep us in our heads, over thinking our next move. When we return to listening to our primal instincts, to feel the rhythm and movement, in this way, we can sense when the time is ripe to burrow to the root of an issue.

PLEASURE AND GUILT

Every word has its connotations, so what do you associate pleasure with? For many people, alongside pleasure, there often comes guilt. Pleasure may seem like a luxury that most people can't afford to have. It may seem frivolous, indulgent, over the top and unnecessary, even narcissistic. Pleasure might actually be at the forefront of the minds of many women. But giving themselves personal pleasures over taking care of relationships and the needs of others first or getting work done may seem inherently selfish and can induce deep feelings of guilt.

We've seen advertising for chocolate placing the words 'guilty' and 'pleasures' together. 'Guilty pleasures' suggest that we should feel guilty about enjoying pleasures like eating chocolate and that there's something inherently naughty about it. Doing naughty and forbidden things might remind us of the feeling of breaking the rules of authority when we were teens. This feeling of breaking free from the confines of control; be that parental, school or governmental authorities can feel gleefully naughty and secretly delightful.

Guilty pleasures are clearly things that give you pleasure, that you also feel guilty about at the same time. Those things are different for each person although there are many common guilty pleasures like chocolate, which many consider indulgent. Guilty pleasures are usually experiences or items we give ourselves, like receiving a massage, buying new shoes, staying in bed all day with your lover, eating high-quality chocolate or taking yourself out for lunch when you didn't get a nice birthday present for your mum, or even watching an uplifting movie. There can often be the idea embedded in your consciousness that something about it is 'bad', even when you know it was enjoyable and gave you so much pleasure. The massage was too self-indulgent, the chocolate was sugary and fattening, the shoes were expensive and unnecessary, you should have used the money on lunch for mums present instead, or watching the movie or staying in bed with your lover was a 'waste of time' and that time could have been spent doing something much more productive or useful. These are the kinds of self-judgemental thoughts that can flow through the mind whilst trying to enjoy something that actually feels pleasurable and that puts us into a good feeling state.

Often guilt is held as tension in the body, so even when we think we're allowing ourselves the pleasure, our pleasure can still become infringed upon by holding tension and thus, we don't fully surrender to the pleasure. There can even be the feeling of anticipation of waiting for the pleasure to leave.

Guilty pleasures are usually different than deeper body melting pleasures; the pleasure part is often ignited *because* we associate them with the memory of being naughty and doing something 'outwith the confines of control'. There is also a moment or a line when the experience of a 'guilty pleasure' can turn to self-sabotage. Melting into the pleasure of slowly eating a dark piece of chocolate with a small glass of pink champagne, while watching a favourite movie; there is a decisive moment. After you have enjoyed these pleasures and feel satiated, you can roll into your cosy bed, happy and contented or eat another two bars of dark chocolate, watch another movie and finish the bottle of champagne. If you choose the latter, not such a pleasurable feeling may follow. There is an art of listening to the knowing and being so present in the moment of pleasure that we honour—a moment that feels so complete.

SACRED OR SECRET?

We often hide our guilty pleasures and keep them secret, worried about what the world may think. We take comfort and find solace in these pleasures alone, keeping them secret for or from ourselves, because of our feelings of shame about them. To be 'secretive' is to be looked upon with a suspicious eye, but not all secrets are bad.

There is something very pleasurable about doing something just for ourselves. Like a special gift, we keep this pleasure close; we keep it sacred because it is a beautiful offering of love to our soul. We do not want to dissipate the energy, taint the experience or be influenced by others judgements and opinions. We want to keep this gift, this delicious pleasure all for ourselves. We want to deeply indulge in our pleasures, because they return us to the earthiness, the physical richness of our bodies and remind us that we are born to experience and enjoy every sensation through them.

There are so many of us that have become familiar with holding some kind of constant tension in the body, that we forget what it feels like, or in the experience of some people, have no conscious recollection of what it feels like, to be completely at peace, at ease, relaxed and surrendered within the body.

We all have our individual struggles in life and when we look around, we can see others struggling in life too; working exhausting, long hours and trying to juggle family, money, career, burnout, disease and ageing parents. We see war, hunger and atrocities on the news every day. Sharing our pleasures with ourselves and others when this is what we feel and see around us can feel like rubbing it in their face and can induce deep guilt.

We are here on the planet to indulge in life itself; the simple *and* extravagant, the worldly, physical, dark, ripe, raw *and* spiritual light-filled pleasures with joyful glee and sacred reverence.

It is in the honouring of who we are and our sacredness that we can accept and receive these experiences, even when struggle and pain are present. Show others by your example that they too deserve to experience whatever they want, because we are sacred creatures who value who we are. Declare it!

SENSUAL PLEASURE

Our bodies are gifts through which we experience all of life. We feel and are felt, we taste, we touch, we smell, we see, we hear, we sense. We embody all of life. Our bodies are made for exploration. To travel us near and far. To be held and to hold, to be stroked and caressed, to be filled and emptied. The greatest pleasure of having a body[6] is to feel the warmth and

---

[6] More on 'body' in chapter 3, Your Body.

adoring touch of another. To enjoy the heightened sensations of physical *and* energetic intimate connection with a beloved. What is considered sensual and sexual pleasure is different for everyone. Some people share an experience that one feels is sensual and another sexual. Sensuality is appreciation through all of the senses and does not need to be sexual in nature, whereas sexuality relates to sex in some way.

Suppressing the desire to joyfully explore sexually often comes from feelings of shame; both of the body and in some way, acknowledging that these feelings even exist. Different cultures and organisations teach us that simply having such natural desires is wrong. When we are taught that our human longings are wrong, it brings up confusion, self-doubt and eventually can lead to a sense of feeling unworthy. We cease to give ourselves the gifts of sexual pleasure. This type of 'education' never leads to a healthy and happy understanding of sex.

Our sexual energy is the energy of creation.[7] **It is life energy.** Through discovering our sexual energy, we also uncover a tremendous source of creative power. And through discovering our creative power, we also tap into our intrinsic sexual energy—because it is the same thing. It is our life-force.

Some women feel their natural sensuality more easily in nature. We can feel the life-force of nature moving through our bodies, softening, yet enlivening us. It can feel both sensual and powerfully sexual. We relax, become more open and feel the inspiration to be creative and to express this life-force energy through our bodies with another or through our creative work.

There are many ways to experience and enjoy your natural sensuality as a woman. In fact, it's possible to feel sensual at any time. We can feel our sensual nature while being softly touched by another or by caress-

---

[7] Read more on sexual energy in chapter 4, Feminine Power.

ing our own bodies. We can feel sensual while eating food, while walking across a room or swimming in a river or ocean. Whether we feel sensual or not in these situations is linked to how connected, relaxed or present we feel in our own bodies.

Take a pen and add your own words to the Pleasure Word Pool below. Meditate on pleasure and ask yourself, 'what does pleasure mean to me?'

delectable ecstasy
gratification exhilaration
amusement melting
Rich Fun! luxury Velvet
excitement (Pleasure) Bliss Joy
Satisfaction delight delicious deep
thrill surrender Plump
Indulge Sensual Comfort Rapture
fulfilment

Life is all encompassing and inter-related. Our creative expressions in life are intrinsically connected to our sexual energy and, therefore, our intimate relationships as well as our work and purpose. Our creative self-expression is woven with our health and wellbeing, our bodies, our love, our relationships and our pleasures. **There is no separation. We only *think* there is.**

THE PLEASURE PROJECT

We like to divide life into distinct categories so that our minds can make sense of things. Structure *is* a good thing and incredibly supportive of many aspects of our lives. Structure offers a container that represents the masculine provider and protector to our feminine flow and inspiration. And although to divide life into categories can help us to clarify and understand things better, it doesn't 'take away' from the fact that all of life is interconnected.

During the course of this book, you'll begin to sense and see new connections between your experiences of pleasure in every area of life. You'll find a Pleasure Project at the end of each chapter to guide you back to your essence and your original joys; to ground you back in your body so that you can make choices based on how you feel. From your body to your creative expression, to home, relationships and nature, the Language of the World can help to guide you every step of the way.

Just as we can easily feel lost finding our way around a new city, town or forest, most of us have felt 'lost' at some point, or many, in our lives. When we are ungrounded, unsure, doubtful, confused and anxious or worried, we can lose trust in ourselves and life itself. Creating Pleasure Projects unique to you, help you to remember, return to or discover what gives you both joy and pleasure and to find the small and large treasures in your days and in your life.

A Pleasure Project is designed to elevate you, to harness the power of your focus, *intention*, *attention* and your energy, on the pleasure and joy in each area of your life. Pleasure Projects can take many forms and because they are unique to you, they will look different for everyone. You will choose how to create your Pleasure Project in the ways that you love the most. If you're not sure what 'ways' these are, you will be by the end of this book.

You can make your very own Pleasure Project journal, one that fits in your bag to go or a giant sketchbook, depending on your style. You can fill your journal with your ideas and inspiration from the Pleasure Projects inside this book. You'll also find a 'notes' section to continue writing your thoughts at the back of this book.

You can create an actual map, a drawing or doodle, have paragraphs painted on paper, make a collage using beloved photos and images from books, magazines or collected things, a giant painting, a series of videos, music or writing. You can dance your pleasure, journal it, sing it, film it or write your notes right here on the pages of this book. This is *your* journey to discover what brings you into this place of pleasure and joy and to witness how the universe listens to your longings.

We will begin with a Pleasure Project to remind you of what brings you pleasure.

PLEASURE PROJECT TIPS

As you progress through this book and engage in each Pleasure Project, you may find that certain chapters or life areas stand out to you more than others. This is natural, so go with it. Notice what gives you pleasure to focus on and what does not, in this moment. What gives you pleasure changes and grows as you proceed, so you can return to each and every project when you want to bring your focus to that life area. You will also want to witness when you find it difficult to focus on an area that may bring up some fear or resistance for you, but that would be very beneficial for you to do. Take note and honour how you may resist and what you tell yourself.

The *Pleasure* Pleasure Project

1. **What gives you that elated, expansive and light feeling of joy? Think about the moments you have felt that way and remember where you were, what you were doing and who you were with.**

Five experiences that make me feel really joyful are:

1.

2.

3.

4.

5.

2. **What surrenders you into blissful, velvety alignment with your pleasure? Think of those moments when you were melting blissfully, what were you doing? Where and who with?**

Five experiences that delve me into my pleasure are:

1.

2.

3.

4.

5.

3. **What pleasures do you enjoy but also feel guilty about at the same time?**

Five guilty pleasures are:

1.

2.

3.

4.

5.

4. **What creates the feeling of guilt when you enjoy these pleasures?**

    Where do you feel the 'root' of these guilty feelings stem from?

You can continue moving into deeper self-inquiry with this question in the notes section or in your journal. However, I suggest reading chapter 6, on Giving and Receiving to support you further with this question since, often our sense of guilt around receiving pleasure is linked to the balance of giving and receiving.

5. **What sacred pleasures do you hold close to your heart that you gift yourself or would like to gift yourself that you do not share with anyone else?**

Five sacred pleasures that I love to gift myself are:

1.
2.
3.
4.
5.

6. **How do you explore or would like to explore your sensual pleasures?**

Five ways I'd love to explore my sensual pleasures are:

1.
2.
3.
4.
5.

Make time for your pleasures, they will nourish you inside and out.

Chapter Summary

- Joy and pleasure are similar, but elicit different states in the body
- Life is meant to be both joyful and pleasurable
- Pleasure is a forgotten language for many women that needs to be re-introduced to all areas of our lives and not just the bedroom!
- More pleasure-filled lives elicit a strong sense of abundance and fruitfulness
- Give yourself the gifts of sacred pleasures to keep just for you
- Activate your natural sensuality through absorbing the energy of nature
- Get yourself a Pleasure Project journal or sketchbook specifically for all the practices you'll learn during the course of this book

Part Two

CHAPTER THREE

The Language of Your Body

Think about this: without your body, where would you be? Our bodies are pretty useful. We do, after all, spend all of our time in them. Even when we're trying to disconnect. They take us places, let us feel things, taste and smell, hear and see things; we connect with other people physically and can grow a human in the female body. Our bodies are spectacular, inexplicably intricate designs and when we learn more about how they work, we discover that we are walking miracles.

It is through our bodies that we experience all of life. Our bodies allow us to actually have a human experience. They are our instruments, whether finely tuned or completely out of tune, well, that's up to us. But the more finely tuned and cared for our instruments are, the better they play and the more pleasure we can experience through them.

Our bodies and how we feel in them are the foundations for a prosperous, vibrant and health-filled life. They are our 'homes'.[8] Without good physical health and wellbeing, other life areas suffer as a result of fragile

---

[8] See chapter 7, Home and Sanctuary for more on body as home.

foundations. Health and wellbeing extend beyond our physical bodies to include mental, emotional, energetic and spiritual health. We are beings made of many facets that create the wholeness of who we are. And each 'part', not separate from the others, affects all 'parts' of us. Just as our experiences in one life area affects all other life areas. Most people do not know all their facets and it is our own responsibility to get to know them. This can be an exciting, mysterious and curious journey of unravelling if we make it so.

Our bodies and all their senses are precious pleasure maps. They are a part of the Language of the World, through which we can experience incredible pleasure and greater clarity when well nourished. Guidance comes to us through our bodies inside and out. The Language of the World is always talking; every moment of life contains a gift and a message.

And so we begin within the *sanctuary* of the body and how we care for our unique 'temples' affects our inner Goddess of Pleasure, our health and our wellbeing on all levels.

BEGINNING YOUR DAY

The very start of your day is an important time. Before the chaos of the world enters, the moment when you awaken, you are still part of Dreamtime and also connected to your innate self. Before your work and responsibilities begin to seep into your personal space, you can breathe and know yourself. You awaken each morning to a new day, to begin it as you like. Your space is your own. This time is the best for attuning to the Language of the World because you are usually more clear and fresh. During your morning practice—more about that below—you can create the intention to be alert and aware of the world as it speaks to you throughout the rest of the day. If you listen to the Language of the World and to your own heart, then you get the best of what the universe can give you that day.

Morning practices can be considered spiritual or self-connecting. They can be used to clear the energetic and emotional 'debris' from day to day so that you can start afresh and feel good about the day ahead. Julia Cameron, author of *The Artists Way,* made famous her 'morning papers'. This was a tool that she used each morning, before she did anything else, to allow free-flow writing; to clear the mental path for the real creative potency to flow. Your practice may involve a physical workout as well as a mental clearing. It needn't be the same every day, however, you should do something that you love and that involves the movement of your body.

What you choose to do may depend on the time slot you have available each morning, what the weather is like outside or on your immediate environment. I'll give you an example of a week of my own morning practices.

On Monday, Tuesday and Wednesday morning, I got up around 7:15 am and went to my living room. I closed the door, put on ambient music and began stretching on a medicine ball. Each morning, I combined breathing with slow movement to music and/or dancing. I did this for around 30-45 minutes, then had a shower, got dressed and made a cup of tea. I then sat down to write this book for 1-2 hours, which also helped me brainstorm ideas for my business. On Thursday morning, I got up at 7:30 am, had breakfast, showered and cycled to a meditation group for a twenty-five-minute meditation. Friday, I was awakened by my housemate calling because she had lost her wallet. While I took the time to search the house for it, she finally announced that she had found it in her car! I then showered and picked an angel card for the day. On Saturday morning, I felt inspired to go for a jog on the beach, as it was a beautiful, sunny, crisp day. Whilst on the beach, I did my slow, intuitive movement practice, which is similar to Tai Chi and generated some ideas for videos. I jogged past a forest with horses penned in and stopped to connect with them for a while. This was the best part of my day! On other days, I've chosen to go for a morning cycle, follow a yoga DVD, go out into the garden and feel the soil beneath my feet, whilst breathing in the fresh morning air, or do a womb connecting practice to ground and centre me in my power source for the day.

As long as you have set the intention to begin the day with yourself and with your connecting practice, you can often decide what it might be in the moment. You may feel inspired to do different things on different days or stick with one practice for the whole week. It's good to sync with your menstrual cycle so that you are following the different energy levels of each phase. Following what inspiration and energy calls you to, is listening to the Language of the Feminine and brings the most pleasure and flow to your days.

I suggest, before you begin your morning practice each day, to start with deep breathing and follow this movement of breath; in through your nose and out down the back of your throat. You will feel the oxygen and energy circulating through your physical body. When you breathe deeply, with awareness, you are inviting more life and energy into you through the breath. Then, take a few moments—depending on how long you have—to tune-in to how you feel physically, emotionally and energetically. In doing so, you are moving your awareness within yourself to connect and listen to your health and wellbeing, through your body, emotions and energy. This will give you clarity as to what morning practice will nourish you the most on different days.

When you start each day this way, you create stillness and space to clearly hear source through the Language of the World talking to you in all the ways that it does. You start the day knowing you, feeling you and listening to you, whilst connected to the central axis inside yourself. The rest of your day, whatever it may hold, will be much more graceful; or rather the way you interact with what happens will be when you've given yourself even five minutes of check-in time.

TOUCH

A playful gust of wind, wildly whisking and flinging your hair over your face can lift you from deep negative thought. Or it may try to. Nature can often be playful, asking for your attention.

A bird pooing on your shoulder may not seem very amusing at the time, but it most likely helped to bring your attention back to the present. Sometimes these 'subtle' ways of the Language of the World physically touching you can return your attention to your body and save you from falling deeper into self-sabotaging or destructive thoughts.

The gentle pressure of a hand on your shoulder or a cat that strolls over and strokes its body on your legs can be a blessing. Animals offer us unconditional love that can be so healing and soothing for our souls. Receiving touch or a warm hug from a friend, family or partner is the Language of the World speaking without words. We can experience incredible pleasure from simple, non-sexual, as well as sexual touch.

The power of being physically touched, whether by another person, an animal, water or the wind, can be incredible. Touch can make us giggle, feel aroused, loved, cared for, nurtured, felt and happy. Touch grounds us on Earth and returns us to the physicality of life. This is especially important for very empathic people, who often feel disconnected from their own bodies, because they feel so much around them.

We often hold so much emotion and tension in the body without being fully aware of it. This is the culmination of so many experiences that were never expressed in the moment, as well as other people's emotional 'stuff' that we can hold unknowingly. Touch is very intimate and so can also make us feel overwhelmed or anxious. For this reason, disconnection can often feel safer than touch. Yet a loving touch or hug contains the power to melt us and our defences, opening the body and allowing this tension to be released.

There are many ways to get back in touch with our bodies and give them the attention they deserve. Ask your partner or a friend for a foot rub, book a massage or bodywork session with someone you feel safe to let go in the presence of, or visit a spa with steam rooms, saunas and a hot tub. Create or join a women's circle or class where sacred, loving touch from other women is often a nurturing component. Plan a juice feast or a cleansing day, clean out your fridge and stock it with living food, ask for a hug and feel the loving warmth of another human. Give yourself loving touch. Stroke your own skin, caress your own hair, and massage your own feet and legs with delicious smelling coconut and essential oils. Explore and get to know your own body. Witness how your body responds to this kind of touch and attention.

BODY TALK

Our bodies are amazing tools of communication. Our physical bodies use a language to speak with our consciousness through illness and disease *and* in more subtle ways. Our bodies contract and tighten when we are stressed, fearful or if we feel we are in danger. When we feel relaxed, at ease, warm, accepting or happy, our bodies release tension and feel more free, limber and open.

If a rash breaks out on the skin, our bodies are speaking with us. There may be a number of factors that contribute to the rash, like emotional stress, toxic skin products or intolerance to certain food. Sometimes, we need to delve a bit deeper to discover what the Language of the World is communicating to us through our bodies. A repetitive illness such as tonsillitis or sore throats may signal the repression of an emotion that is deeply important for us to communicate, or our bodies may simply ask that we look inward and be in silence for a while. We must unravel the messages in illness for ourselves, as their cause and meaning will differ according to the individual.

There are a wonderful variety of books that can help us to understand and find the emotional and mental root causes of disease and illness including *Women's Bodies, Women's Wisdom*[9] by Dr. Christiane Northrup and *Heal Your Body, Heal Your Life* by Louise L. Hay which is now also available as an A-Z app called *The Mental Causes of Physical Illness and the way to Overcome them.*[10]

I suggest before reading these books, that you sit in stillness and tune-in to your own body first. Meditate upon the ailing part and ask why it is there and what it wants to tell you about yourself. You might receive an intuitive message, through an image, a word, a feeling or simply a deep knowing about the meaning of this illness. By doing this practice first, you begin to build a relationship of trust with your body and your own intuition. You can then follow up on your own feelings by researching different mental, emotional and spiritual roots of an illness or disease.

Our bodies are communicating with us in every moment. If we take the time to ask and if we listen, our bodies will always tell us their wants

[9] Northrup, Dr. Christiane, *Women's Bodies, Women's Wisdom—The Complete Guide to Women's Health and Wellbeing.*

[10] Heal Your Body A-Z App—Louise L. Hay - http://www.oceanhousemedia.com/products/healyourbody/&legacy/.

and needs. Usually, the reason we get the illness in the first place is be-cause we *don't* listen to our bodies' distress calls. Our bodies are their own genius and deserve great respect and appreciation for carrying us through this journey of life.

MOVING YOUR BODY

Focusing awareness on your physical body can help to ground you, bring you into the present moment *and* feel more pleasure. By moving and stretching your body, you move energy, through your focus, to the different parts of your physicality. You will begin to feel where you have unconsciously been holding tension.

Rather than sitting in the traditional way to meditate, movement itself can become the meditation. Your daily life can be one constant moving meditation. When you *do* move, to walk somewhere, stretch or dance a little, focus on your body and its movement; go within and enjoy being in your body. This is your meditation.

A large percentage of the adult population now spend the majority of their time sitting stationary behind a computer, day after day, occasionally getting up to make a cup of tea. Continuous sitting for hours at a time can contribute to bad posture, repetitive strain injuries and is linked to the development of Type 2 diabetes. It can also lead to depression, being overweight and feeling unhealthy and disconnected from life. In this type of work environment, it can be easy to forget how it actually feels to feel physically vital and alive and how to feel pleasure, by just 'being' in your body.

I received a wonderful reminder of the wisdom and necessity of move-ment from the Language of the World through two young teenage boys. I'd like to share this short story here to inspire you to get physical every day and the results that can happen when you do:

One sunny, fresh spring afternoon, I sat at a wooden picnic table on the banks of an amber coloured river in the highlands of Scotland. I was happily eating my picnic lunch and drinking warm tea from my flask when I heard voices behind me. I turned around, cup of tea in hand, and saw two young boys around the age of fourteen, clambering down the very steep slope on the opposite side of the river. Previously, there had been a landslide there and the soil was loose and crumbly. Their youthful exuberance was magnetic and I watched them laughing together and mucking around, whilst thinking to myself, "It's a bit dangerous to be climbing down a steep slope with such loose soil". After a few moments, my hunger turned me back to my picnic and to my voice recorder, in which I was recording ideas and inspiration for this book. A few moments later, I was distracted from my notes when I heard the two boys' laughter suddenly much louder than before. I was surprised when I turned around to find them climbing the small slope right behind me on the same side of the river I was on. In the couple of minutes I had my back turned, they walked over a fallen tree trunk that was balanced over the river to the other side, and it seems they had a lot of fun doing it. I could feel their exhilaration and energy from the excitement of doing something challenging and achieving it, bolstered on by each other. Their vitality and enthusiasm were contagious. Not only did they remind me of what it felt like to be a young teenager, they helped to propel my own thoughts and sense of enthusiasm towards how good it feels to stretch myself physically and that my body is capable of so much more than I think.

The more present and embodied we are, the more present we are in our lives to what is happening in the here and now. The fourteen-year-old boys in my story reminded me of how good it feels to be fully in *my* body and of the boundless energy many children have that seems to diminish as life progresses.

MOVING TO CONNECT WITH THE DIVINE

There are many styles of dance, movement and physical practices that are designed to take us into a meditative state and to develop a connection with our divine nature.

Many indigenous dances from around the world use movement with music to connect the dancer to their inner source. The sacred Hula Dance from Hawaii is a carefully choreographed dance that is designed to connect the dancer with spirit or God *and* to teach and emotionally move audiences. Salsa and sensual dance can help us to explore the deeply sensual and erotic aspects of ourselves. Movement and dance can be transformational as we connect simultaneously with our physical bodies and with our deepest source, whilst experiencing great pleasure. **Movement and dance are part of our pleasure map to life.**

When we physically and practically do these types of movement we have an embodied experience, rather than just an intellectual one. We can feel the experience in the body and 'know' it in a way that is not possible solely through the mind. Embodiment makes experience three dimensional. Embodiment brings colour, shape, depth, energy and vibrancy to intellectual concepts, which although can be stimulating and energising, are a two-dimensional experience without body connection.

You may already do something regularly that you naturally love; like going for a long run, walking in nature or going to salsa classes, which you don't particularly think of as a 'spiritual' practice. And yet doing it connects you to clarity and a sense of pleasure within and often a feeling of connectivity to the people and the world around you. This is a beautiful example of how following your pleasure and doing the things you love to do, brings you into the same place of connectivity, clarity and love with more ease, grace and joy, than say, forcing yourself to sit in a half lotus meditation pose on the floor for an hour trying to be 'spiritual'.

You are spiritual already; your existence makes it so.

There are so many body-based movement practices that we can experience; each one involves different kinds of body movement that enhance different mental, emotional and energetic states of being. Different body movements also bring us into a more masculine or feminine energy. During my life I've practiced slow intuitive deliberate movement, like an intuitive version of Tai Chi or Qi Gong, yoga in many forms, Chakra, 5Rhythm and ecstatic dance, contact improvisation, hip-hop, salsa and sensual dance, running, nature hikes, cycling, swimming, capoeira, snowboarding and skiing, amongst other things.

Within the realm of yoga, each person enters into the practice with a different intention. There is holiness to certain branches of yoga, in that they offer an opportunity to connect with the divine through the body and listen carefully to her language. Combined with the breath, yoga can support entering into a place of stillness, whilst staying flexible in body and attitude.

As with any practice, the important thing is that you really enjoy it. Don't do it because you think you should if it doesn't entice you. If you turn up at your weekly yoga class with dread and spend the whole class cursing the yoga teacher in your mind and thank God when it's over, you're not benefitting anyone, especially yourself.

Your body benefits from experiencing a variety of movement practices, such as the slow stretch of yoga, the feminine flow or wild chaos you can find through 5Rhythm dance, the erotic embodiment of sensual dance or the focused, muscular and masculine movement and speed of skiing. Exploring this range helps us to feel the contrast between them and the different 'states' they bring us into which we can use during the different stages of our lives. This helps us to understand the language of our bodies. However, for *most* women who want to experience deeper pleasure through their bodies, it is the feminine forms of movement that will bring them there.

MOVING WITH MASCULINE AND FEMININE ENERGY

There are people who experience a lot of pleasure from extreme sports, the pleasure of danger, the thrill of being on the edge, because it makes them feel *alive*. Skydiving, triathlons, running a marathon, jumping out a helicopter to ski down a high mountain ridge, white water kayaking; participating in these sports all get adrenalin pumping through the body, which activates the feeling of being alive.

This feeling can be addictive, like a drug, there is an extreme high, the thrill and excitement—the danger element. This heightened kind of exhilarating pleasure and 'go-go-go' energy is difficult and exhausting to maintain long term. Staying in this state for prolonged periods of time can eventually lead to adrenal burnout, leaving a feeling of depletion or flatness.

These sports can also enhance and activate the masculine essence within us. The masculine essence, just like the feminine essence has many 'flavours' in that there are many forms of expression within the spectrum of these energies. And when two strong opposing energies meet, they create polarity.

Feminine pleasure is a whole other pleasure game because this kind of pleasure comes with a deep relaxation, grounding and connection to the body. Movement that cultivates the feminine essence and a feminine state of being includes various forms of dance, such as salsa, belly dance and sensual dance. These forms of dance bring us into the lower half of the body, the hips, the belly, the solar plexus, the pelvic bowl and the womb. These are the power and sexual centres of the female body, in which feminine essence can be activated and cultivated. When you bring your attention to your womb area, you will, over time, tune-in to the powerful language and wisdom that she holds.[11]

In 5Rhythm dance, we can explore the range of masculine and feminine movements as we ride the wave of movement and music from flowing to staccato, chaos to lyrical to stillness. This dance is called 'movement meditation' or movement medicine and was originally devised by Gabrielle Roth, in the late 1970s. Roth has said that practicing the dance puts the body in movement to still the mind. To embody the five rhythms of the dance is to access the deep internal wisdom that is contained within the body. A key, if you will, to 'unlock' the knowing of the body.

You already have seeds of ancient wisdom and knowledge within you, held in your physical body, ready to be revealed and coaxed out. When you learn to listen to the guidance of *your* body, to feel and understand your *own* energy system and how to intuitively work with it for yours and others benefit; you begin to build incredible confidence, self-assurance and self-trust in your own abilities and inner knowing. It cultivates a 'you can do it' (and you already know how) attitude when you learn to use your body as a map, listen to its language and let it be your guide to pleasure.

---

[11] See more on this in chapter 4, Feminine Power.

The *Body* Pleasure Project

BEGINNING YOUR DAY

Begin your self-connecting/spiritual practice every morning this week. Even if it means getting up 30 minutes earlier than usual, it will be worth it! If you are not sure what you can do, here is a list of practices that will help inspire you to choose:

- Sit in stillness and focus on your breathing (5-30 mins.)
- Sit in stillness whilst listening to tranquil music (like Native American flute or sounds of nature) and allow the music to take you on a journey
- Do a slow intuitive movement practice with tranquil music and allow your body to move very slowly, guided by your intuition and breath
- Do the slow intuitive movement practice outside in nature
- Dance to music
- Go for a nature walk (taking your dog for a walk or visiting an animal is also wonderful)
- Go for a jog
- Follow a guided meditation
- Do some yoga (follow a DVD, go to an early morning class in your area or do your own practice at home)
- Breathe and stretch on a medicine ball
- Do some sound making and toning.[12] (Great for opening the

[12] Watch my interview with sound, voice and toning expert, Jill Purce to learn more about sound here: http://www.janecormack.com/video-audio/.

voice and the throat chakra, especially if you have to do a lot of speaking during the day)

- Write in your journal/take time to capture last night's dream
- Free-flow write in your journal for 10 minutes
- Sing acapella or sing to music, whilst making a green smoothie
- Go to a group meditation in your area
- Pick an Angel Oracle card (a huge variety of beautiful cards are available at many alternative bookstores, I like Angels, Gods & Goddesses by Toni Carmine Salerno)

MOVING WITH MASCULINE AND FEMININE ENERGY

1. **What forms of movement do you enjoy that bring you into a more masculine state of being?**

2. **How do you feel when you are in that state of being?**

3. **What forms of movement do you enjoy that bring you into a more feminine state of being?**

4. **How do you feel when you are in that state of being?**

> *Tips > Film yourself doing a sensual dance to music you love then watch it and notice what you feel.*
>
> *Combine paint and colour with movement and music, get your body involved and make your mark on paper!*

Love what you do! Start the day with self-love and you will experience more pleasure during the moments of your day. You'll also have more to give and share when you have given yourself this gift first.

▪ Chapter Summary

- Begin each day with a morning practice that connects you to your body and lets you feel your emotions
- Physical touch can be powerful and a gift to bring you back to the present moment
- Your body is an amazing tool of communication and lets you know in every moment its needs and desires; listen to it!
- Get physical! Keep your body moving in different ways to avoid stagnant energy
- Different forms of movement can bring you into a more masculine or feminine state
- Moving in ways that activate the feminine energy in your life is a powerful way to experience deeper pleasure
- If you want to activate more masculine energy in your body and life, try some of the sports suggested in this chapter

CHAPTER FOUR

The Language of Feminine Power

Women's bodies are designed to receive, to experience fullness and pleasure. Our feminine forms are physically beautiful in all their variety of shapes, sizes and colours; soft, lithe, lean, voluptuous, freckled, pink, shining black, olive, neat and petite and bountiful. Our variety is vast and yet we all contain and have access to the same source of feminine power. In many women, this power still lies dormant, waiting to be awakened and experienced. We must learn to access and embrace it for ourselves with the support of our sisters. The Language of the World has brought this book to you. Treat it as a message, a seedling or a catalyst that guides you into the awakening of your feminine wholeness, essence and power.

FEMININE RHYTHM

Women have a natural internal rhythm that changes during any given month. Dr Christiane Northrup, author of the bestselling book, *Women's Bodies, Women's Wisdom*, says that the macrocosmic cycles of nature are reflected on a smaller scale in the menstrual cycle of the female body.

A woman's body can be so in tune with the rhythm of nature that our menstrual cycles can and will adjust in accordance with it. Many cultures view our cycle as sacred. However, in western cultures, it has not been commonly seen this way. Most women from these cultures have not been taught to be aware of their own natural rhythm and have forgotten how to listen to their bodies and the immense wisdom that is contained there. Mainstream media continually tells us that having our period is a nuisance and gets in the way of us being able to live a 'normal' life. It shows us ways to block, stifle or stop our monthly cycles altogether so that we can, y'know, go rock-climbing or something and keep on going, keep on working, keep on doing, don't stop! What mainstream media doesn't show us is how to respect, honour and listen to our bodies. We are not taught about the incredible gifts and power that we have access to within the womb and about our intricate hormonal systems. Our current learning must come from other, alternative forms.

When we listen to the wisdom of the womb, we can hear the language of our physical and energetic bodies. It is the Language of the World speaking to us *through* our bodies. Our wombs are grounding, centring and powerful forces within us; they are powerful organs of perception. Through this feminine element, we perceive life in a different way. Our feminine essence opens up an entire realm of sensations that speak with us, just like a language. This may at first seem chaotic yet, if we listen, we can begin to understand our feminine wholeness through the language of sensations. Our wombs, in connection with our hearts and whole body hold the key to our personal transformation into the feminine, whole, powerful, wise, confident and creative women that we are inside, yet have found difficult to *be*. Cultivating a strong connection in particular to our wombs (or womb space if you have no physical womb) *and* our hearts can offer a foundation for a fulfilling, creative and abundant life.

The womb is the seat of creation within all women yet this most precious gift is often acutely under-recognised. Instead of nurturing, respecting and listening to this wisdom, many women ignore or suppress their vast creative energy and feminine desires, as I myself have done in the past. As young women, most of us were not taught how to communicate, listen and experience true pleasure in our own bodies or how to utilise the energetic power of our womb. Nor were most women taught to have any understanding of the connection between our wombs and feminine rhythms to the 'womb' or centre of this planet and the rhythms of nature.

STRESS

Developing a strong womb connection is especially important if we experience a lot of stress in our lives, because it returns us to our internal centre of power, stillness and strength. If we are 'plugged-in' to the internet, phone and social media 24/7, it can cause over-stimulation of our senses. We are also negatively affected by the Wi-Fi waves of energy that now surround us in our homes, cafes, universities and schools, which can drain our energy. We become disconnected from the wisdom of our bodies and hearts and do not feel grounded. Too much plugged in time makes us feel 'heady', because all of our focus and thus energy is around our heads. This can result in being 'flighty', easily distracted, stressed, not very present in the company of others and forgetting about self-care.

Technology gives us freedom and power and supports us in our social and professional lives; but we must learn to balance our time spent connected to the virtual world, with time spent connected to our own bodies, our innate inner wisdom and the natural world. If you sit at a computer all day, then take regular ten-minute breaks to look around and re-connect with what's in your immediate environment.

Return now to the connection with your own present moment reality; wherever you are, whatever you are doing right now, look around you. Look at the table you may sit at, the cup of tea you hold in your hands, feel the warm liquid moving through your body, feel your buttocks resting on the chair, look closely at the vase of pink and yellow flowers on the windowsill and how the cloud-filtered sunlight highlights the fine veins of certain petals, listen to the sound of the rain falling through tree canopies outside or feel the warmth of the sun through your conservatory window.

What do your ears hear? Listen to the moment. What do you feel in your body right now? Enjoy the sensation of whatever it is you are doing in the environment you find yourself in.

THE CREATIVE FEMININE

Just as the seasons ebb and flow, we need time to integrate our experiences and to go within. We need time to reflect equally as much as producing and pouring our creation energy outward into what we want to create. Creation energy is our life-force and the energy of source. In Chinese medicine, they call it *Qui*. It is the flow of energy within our bodies. Creation energy is the same energy used to heal and to create the projects we work on. It is our sexual energy and it's what gives us momentum and drive to create what we want in our lives. Learning to circulate this energy within our bodies amplifies our life-force energy and our inner fire.

We can easily dissipate this energy in so many different ways through dysfunctional eating, over-talking or over-exercising. However, try to first contain this amazing life-force energy within and feel the pleasure in having it move around your body. Then, with consideration, choose something that is important to you that you would like to channel this energy into. What creative projects, relationships or experiences would you like to grow and flourish? As you do this, you will begin to witness yourself, your work or relationships change and then thrive.

Creation energy is the infinite source of energy available in the universe from the source which you carry within your own being. We are the creation 'babies' of source and, therefore, we create using the same energy. Much like the cycle of breathing in and out, of giving and receiving, we are created and we create. In women, the most potent creative force is found within the womb. With this creation energy, we can create new life in the form of a child. We create the design of our lives and we can also create our ideas and projects, be that a silver and glass ring, a handmade book of poetry or an online course on love and relationships. The projects we create need our consistent nurturance, love and attention during the period of time we mould them into shape. They are our creation 'babies'. How do you want them to grow? When nurtured, our projects can grow into well-balanced, giving and loving creations that radiate and shine from the attention they have received. Yet without our nurturing we may never let them go or produce creations that are chaotic, confused, unbalanced and un-grounded.

All of our creations have their own energy. Your creations are an *extension* of your energy. We birth them and raise our creative projects to a certain point, which can mirror a similar relationship in raising our children to adulthood. And so we must also cut the umbilical cord of our creations and let them go out into the world, allowing them to blossom without any expectations of what they will become, just as we should with our children when they have reached maturity. When we release our creations, they have a chance to discover who or what they are. We take off the limitations and let them breathe.

We let them become something more than they could be if we continued to hold onto them. We allow our creations to morph and change and then we give ourselves the freedom to move on in our lives and to let in the new.

When we cut that umbilical cord we are giving the greatest gift a creator can give its 'children'. We can watch in awe as our creative projects and our children become something magical that we could never have anticipated. We watch as they grow and flourish, our creativity weaving its way through the world and our children finding out who they are for themselves.

WOMEN'S WISDOM

It's become common practice for women to suppress, push down and ignore their own internal wisdom and creative feminine guidance. Many women learnt to suppress their wild, instinctive natures and to drown out the guiding voices from within in order to 'fit in' to society. The culture that we were raised in dictates to a large extent what is acceptable to be and what is not. Many of us, through no fault of our own or of our parents, were not taught to trust ourselves and to embrace the wilder, darker aspects of our characters that contribute to the wholeness of who we are. The denial and fear of our own power contributes to the denial of our 'wholeness', which is what can cause us so much pain.

When we suppress something, we are not listening to some aspect of what we feel. Long-held suppression causes undue problems on all levels. Physically, it can lead to illness and disease, emotionally and psychologically it can lead to bitterness and volcanic rage, to various levels of severity of depression and mental problems.

For many years, I suffered terribly each month on the first day of my menstrual cycle. I gradually came to realise that there were several contributing factors that would either lead me to have a deep and restfully nourishing time on my first day or a painful and horrific experience. I eventually began to understand that having a menstrual cycle is a gift and that aligning my daily life to move in unison with this natural rhythm each month, made life more pleasurable, insightful and enjoyable in every way. An emotionally stressful month with little nurturing, relaxation and rejuvenation time would lead towards extreme pain. If I lived in a busy, congested and polluted environment where I was over-stimulated and overwhelmed and I didn't protect myself daily with strong boundaries and deep self-care, it would result in a 'purging' during the first day of my cycle. My body would spend one day ridding itself of the accumulation of energetic, emotional and physical build up that had created blockages during the month. It was painful and exhausting, but often, the following day, although I still felt very delicate, I would also feel cleaner and clearer emotionally, mentally and physically. But I really didn't want to experience such extreme measures in order to reach that place of clarity!

By contrast, if I had spent plenty of time in nature, connecting with loved ones, expressing myself creatively, eating nourishing food, doing regular exercise and staying grounded within my body; my first day would be deeply restful and a time to move deeper within myself to listen.

In our modernised culture, most women do not stop to rest during this time and it is hurting them. No time is taken to feel and to process the experiences of the previous 28 days or to release the emotional and energetic accumulation of what has happened so that we can clear space ready for the month ahead. In our modern culture, there seems to be no time to do that which is most natural and that which supports a woman to be, give and do of her best from her most potent power through the month. I personally know, all too well, the suffering that this can cause.

Our monthly menses is our nectar from the hive of our wombs. If we care for ourselves very well, particularly prior to menstruation, when we begin to bleed, like nectar, we can harvest a multitude of the sweetest, most potent, inspired ideas and clear intuitive 'knowing' from a place of deep wisdom. Sensitivity is heightened so we can access deeper insights that we often feel under the surface during the rest of the month but don't always hear as clearly. This is the feminine power within. Now it arises and if we give ourselves space, time to reflect, go outside, be in nature and do what the soul is calling us to do, which also may be nothing, we are acting in reverence of our GOD-dess nature. We treat this time and ourselves as sacred. Because it is.

This is a window of opportunity each month to truly listen and to let go of what we no longer need; this happens physically, emotionally and energetically during the menses.

To live a life in congruence with *your* natural rhythm, slow down and listen to the language of your body; it has so much to tell you and so much pleasure to offer. We must learn to cultivate patience and that means being gentle with ourselves. Giving ourselves what we need in gifts of love, time and space, nature walks, warm baths, early nights or dinner with friends. Giving ourselves these gifts of nurturing helps us to return to our natural selves and the wisdom we hold. When we give ourselves these gifts first, we are better able to shine and play our part in making a difference in this world and to fully enjoy all aspects of our lives. We can teach younger generations of girls to love and care for themselves and to cherish the gifts their monthly cycles bring, so that they begin to sense the power and beauty of becoming a woman, rather than feel the pain and fear passed on from suffering mothers. We can offer a more nourishing environment so that these girls can grow into powerful and feminine women.

RITES OF PASSAGE

Women's bodies are inherently connected to the 'body' of Earth and to the moon. When we enter deep into the wisdom of our womb on our first days of menstruation, we have the ability to access a consciousness that is connected to the living, breathing centre of this planet. **We have an ability to access a level of depth and power way beyond what we imagine to be possible.** Our wombs are filled with possibility and are the centre of our own internal universe. This monthly gift needs to be re-learnt and understood by all women so that we can utilise this powerful time and pause to acknowledge our much larger connection to nature.

In many indigenous cultures of North America, Australia and Africa, women would gather together at a sacred site in nature; a 'red tent' or hut, specifically made for menstruating and birthing women. Each month around the onset of menstruation, women would have time away from their families and responsibilities to gather together, re-connect with the wisdom of their bodies and share stories from their lives.

Thankfully we now have the 'Red Tent Movement' growing across the world. Red Tents can be actual tents, huts, studios or homes chosen and created by women as a dedicated gathering place around the full and new moon for women to come to be together during menstruation. The spaces are created by women for women to support each other, share, listen, rest, nourish and allow the body and soul to replenish. Red Tents are rooted in tribal cultures and in ancient Christian history where sacred gathering places were created for women to birth and to bleed. Many original gathering places were actually created by men so that they could send the women away during this time.

In traditional Native American cultures, girls were honoured in their journey into womanhood when their physical bodies announced the onset of becoming a woman through menstruation. Sacred ceremony and celebration symbolised the new spiritual and physical closeness of the girl to Mother Nature. Her transformation reflects the bounty and fertility of Mother Earth, as she enters into her new life as wife and mother to be. For women in the modern world, we can choose to use the energy of this fertile bounty in so many creative ways other than giving birth to a child.

In indigenous cultures, boys often go through a rite of passage into manhood. This passage can involve many challenges that test their physical, emotional and spiritual strength, as well as their quickness of thought and wit. Situations can be dangerous and life threatening, but those boys find out what they are made of. If they emerge unscathed or even a little scathed, they grow tremendously in self-confidence, assurance, pride and trust. They gain respect from their peers and are ready to pass through the invisible doors from child to young man.

These rites of passage have been lost over time in most of today's modern culture. The transformation from child to adult is often hidden away and passed through in private, rather than being acknowledged and celebrated for the experience that it is. Natural life progressions, such as 18th and 21st birthday celebrations, first sexual experiences or a GAP year, travelling the world after finishing high school, can be considered some modern forms of rites of passage, which are authentic to the culture of the people who practice them. Yet, whether they are viewed as rites of passage or treated as sacred experiences is entirely an individual choice.

WHAT IS A POWERFUL WOMAN?

A woman realising her innate power can be considered a rite of passage as she both claims and connects to this force within. A powerful woman is one who is deeply connected to herself. She is a woman who listens and takes action upon the internal guidance she feels. A powerful woman can emanate a magnetically palpable presence without saying a word. She can be surrounded by chaos and be at peace inside herself because she knows she has access to the source within her and all around her. She knows that she *is* the source. She knows that her compassion, love, gentleness, strength, feminine beauty, grace, joy, anger, passion, her shadows and darkness *are* her power.

A powerful woman can go unnoticed because she chooses to. She can blend into the trees in a forest or she can stand on a stage with a spotlight shining on her, sharing her wisdom, her humour and passion to a captivated audience.

Many women are still scared of their own power. They have learnt to give it away, to disempower themselves because they do not want to own it. They don't know how to access it, be it or what to do with it because no one ever taught them. They are afraid of their own power and the infinite mystery of it.

The word 'power' when connected to 'woman' often conjures the image of a feisty, mouthy, pushy, loud, driven and sometimes scary woman. The same woman may be described as passionate, expressive, bold, focused and clear, conjuring a very different, more positively focused image. Yet, the power of women is not always visible. And, the most gentle and quietest of women can be powerful.

There is extreme pleasure in accessing and owning our own power. When we know it's there, when we're not afraid of it, it's like a delicious secret that can unfold graciously or strike like lightning at any moment.

A powerful woman knows she has the power to choose; how to be, where to be or who to be, if she listens. Her internal language is the Language of the World speaking from within, through her feelings and her body. And outside she witnesses the world speaking to her through colour, sound, story, music and people; all the things that she loves. She is life and life moves through her. When we accept this power, we can learn to enjoy it and truly feel pleasure in this aspect of ourselves.

Tip > Plumping up your pleasure has everything to do with being in touch with your feminine essence.

The *Feminine Power* Pleasure Project

WOMB CONNECTION[13]

This basic womb connection exercise will bring you into connection with your womb so that you can begin to feel and listen to her wisdom. If you have never fully connected to your womb before now, then you may expect to feel some kind of emotional release. Allow this to happen as it is a natural part of the process. You may want to take some time to write in your Pleasure Project journal about your experience. Take at least 15 minutes or more to do this exercise.

You can try either of the following positions for this exercise. Each position will ignite slightly different sensations:

Position 1: Sit comfortably on the floor with the soles of your feet together and your knees spread outwards.

Position 2: Stand with your feet firmly rooted on the floor and your knees slightly bent so that your legs are not locked. Let your shoulders drop and relax your jaw and your facial muscles.

---

[13] Inspired and adapted from 'The Art of Feminine Presence™' Level 1 Practices workbook, 2010-2012, by Rachael Jayne Groover with permission.

Close your eyes. Place your hands over your womb area in an inverted triangle so that your thumbs meet at your belly button and your fingers meet 3 inches below it. This is the centre point of your womb. Breathe in deeply and as you breathe out, feel your breath move down into your pelvic bowl with your attention behind where your fingers meet, inside your body.

Continue to breathe into your womb, giving her your full attention. Let all of your conscious awareness go into her and feel your breath filling your whole pelvic bowl area. You can also imagine a light glowing inside your womb space that grows brighter and stronger with each breath you flow into her, until your whole womb space is filled with this light and energy. Notice what you feel and allow yourself to experience what may be new sensations for you.

Your womb has a voice, listen to what she has to say. You are learning the language of your womb.

Write in your journal the wisdom that you receive when you listen to her. This may come in the form of body or energetic sensations, images, words, emotions or an intuitive knowing.

Chapter Summary

- Women's bodies are designed for pleasure
- Women have a natural internal rhythm that is our menstrual cycle
- Women's menstrual cycles can and will adjust in accordance with nature
- Listen to the wisdom held within your womb
- Take regular ten minute breaks to avoid stress and to reconnect with your body and your present surroundings
- You are wise!
- Make peace with your menstrual cycle and learn to use the gifts of each phase to your advantage
- Utilise the power of your menstrual cycle to fuel your creative projects and release them into the world
- Live in congruence with your natural rhythm
- Embrace your unique feminine power

CHAPTER FIVE

The Language of Love and Relationships

Often we are blind to the true magnificence of each other—to seeing the infinite and whole being who stands before us, vulnerable and strong, an intricate map of history and presence, of raw humanity and pure divinity.

Most of us want to be seen beyond our outer appearance, beyond the choices we have made in the past, the age we are at, the work we are doing or the money we have or don't have.

What other people think about us can be particularly challenging to feel for highly sensitive empaths. It can feel deflating to realise that the 'you' your friend, sibling or father sees, is not the person that you know yourself to be. They see the 'you' they think you are through the filters of their own beliefs and perceptions. It can feel constricting to be cemented in someone's eyes this way, yet most people do this, most of the time.

We all need to be around people who accept and trust that we are capable of anything, who are curious to know us and who are believers in the infinite possibilities and magic of life; then we stand in the field of that infinite relationship. In this place, we feel accepted just as we are now, yet also expansive and free to become more.

Equally, if we are in the presence of someone who does not fully 'see' us, who judges us and may think we are selfish, have put on too much weight and probably shouldn't wear a skirt that tight; then we may find ourselves not feeling so good or a little uncomfortable when we are with them. *We* feel what *they* are thinking and feeling about us and oftentimes actually conform to their perceptions without fully realising it. It's not until we are outwith their presence that we can see how differently we might have been behaving. How we feel about ourselves and how well we know ourselves can determine how much we allow this to affect us.

Who you choose to spend time with is important.

Discovering who you are is empowering and allows you to be more present in your self-knowing in the company of others. Through developing personal boundaries, you can feel centred and in touch with what you feel and how others feel without taking on their stuff.

We can often feel triggered by people who unintentionally or intentionally push our 'buttons', yet these people help us to see our limiting thoughts and judgements about ourselves and others. So every 'messenger' brings the perfect gift, at the perfect time, reflecting exactly where we are in the moment.

VARIETY OF RELATIONSHIP

We have so many varieties of relationships with others, although the term 'Love and Relationships' commonly brings to mind romantic love and intimacy for most people. You had a relationship with your school teachers, with your childhood friends, your classmates at University, with your parents, your brothers and sisters, your housemates, perhaps your students if you teach or your colleagues and employees, your great auntie that you visit twice a year, your personal and professional mentors and every person you make a connection with each day, including the man who serves you coffee at the bookstore. We also have a relationship with the Earth herself and with nature.[14] We have relationships with the animals in our lives and the plants we take care of. Anything that we connect with, we also form a relationship with. Whether that connection lasts for three seconds while making eye contact with someone, or three decades of journeying together matters not. Our lives revolve around relationships, they change our lives, create impact and meaning, influence our direction and often the way we perceive the world.

YOU

The primary relationship you have throughout life is with yourself. In every moment, you are with yourself. You can never leave 'you'. Each of us have a relationship with the wholeness of who we are and with the many different aspects of who we are. You have a relationship with the sweet, compassionate, loving aspect of your nature that probably feels different from the relationship you have with the powerful, angry, outspoken aspect of your nature. And most people favour the socially acceptable, 'happy' aspects of themselves more than the darker 'less acceptable' aspects.

There are probably parts of your body you love and parts you wish were different too. Those parts of our bodies have received constant judgement and criticism from us throughout our lives for not being enough—whether it's not smooth enough, thin enough, plump enough, dark or light enough, tall or short enough or toned enough. Parts of us have received our 'not enough' criticisms for long enough. Those parts deserve better from us. They deserve our respect and love. Our bodies carry us through the journey of life. Let us treat them well, as we might a dear friend.

---

[14] Read more on this in chapter 6, Home and Sanctuary.

Take time to get to know who you are, what you need, what environment, food, people and experiences make you thrive. Love yourself by listening. Listen to the language of your emotions, the language of what you feel, what you want, the language of your body and the language of your energy and intuition.

**Each situation and experience we find ourselves in reflects
the relationship that we have with ourselves.**

Low self-worth is prevalent in western culture and it keeps people making choices for their lives that are not based on love. They are choices based on an internal sense of value and worth. If we don't know and love ourselves, then we make choices that reflect that. Like living in an environment that doesn't support who we are, choosing unhealthy food or abusive, draining relationships or even wearing clothes that look and feel 'safe'. When we try to hide who we are and how we feel, we also dampen how we show up in life.[15]

The life we live shows us exactly how we feel about ourselves. We attract what we need, even if that means we keep attracting what we don't really want. When we've had enough of attracting what we don't really want, the question arises, why? Why does this experience keep showing up? I want something different. When we fall in love with ourselves and treat ourselves well, we raise the standard of how others treat us, because we show them by example how we would like to be treated. That's when we begin to make new choices that determine a new path because we have claimed our value and know our worth. **We are born with worth intact and leave the planet with it intact, our worth is intrinsic to who we are and it is non-negotiable.**

---

[15] See chapter 9, Colour and Creating Yourself for more on this.

MESSENGERS

The Language of the World is no more potently spoken than through people. The answer to our questions, wants and desires can arrive out the blue, through a few words with a stranger, through the passing on of a book, an e-mail, a letter, a gift, a smile or a video, an online course or a workshop event. We can and do receive the greatest gifts from the universe through our fellow humans. We are all messengers and agents of change. We are all guides for each other, sometimes without ever realising it.

Everyday messengers can appear to simply lift us from our repetitive or negative patterns of thought, to quickly shift our perspective. I share one such example here:

I had just returned from living overseas and was back at my parents' house in Scotland, in winter. I was broke, in debt and not sure how I was going to get myself out of it. I was none too pleased about my situation and falsely felt like there was nothing exceptionally 'positive' going on in my life at that moment, so I went out for a walk to connect with nature. I walked around the muddy fields near the house cursing at the dull, grey climate and slopping through the mud in my welly boots whilst mulling over how awful my situation was. I felt completely in resistance to my current circumstances. I looked up to see what I thought was a deer standing at the top of the slope in the distance. As I moved closer I saw that it was actually a dog; an elegant, grey deerhound. I walked towards the animal and as I did, the owner, a man in his mid-sixties wearing olive green wellies and a tweed cap, appeared behind it over the slope. As we walked towards each other, a smaller greyhound also appeared by his side. The man greeted me with incredible enthusiasm. "Isn't this marvellous!" he said. "Look at that, where do you get a view like this for FREE!?" he said, waving his arm towards the sea. "The ocean right there, the big sky, fresh air, what a glorious day!" I looked around me. He was right, it was a glorious day and I was alive, healthy and well, to see it and be in it. He had immediately brought my attention back to the present moment. We stood and chatted for some time while we watched his beautiful dogs running over the fields and playing together and then we went our separate ways. I left them feeling completely uplifted, which helped me to change my perspective and be more open to new solutions for my then life situation.

We may never know the true impact our actions have on others by simply being and expressing who we are. To give of our natural personality, whether that be our humour, charm, affection, empathy, knowing, determination, creativity or clarity, may be just the gift someone needs in that moment.

MENTORS AND ENTRAINMENT

We can hire a professional mentor to be our coach in business or relationship but mentors often arrive naturally when we need a guide in life. The mentor relationship is usually longer term and a person in which we trust to offer us the wisdom and guidance from their own similar experiences. Mentors often act as a bridge to support us moving into new unknown terrain.

We mentor and teach each other by example. Therefore, we are all mentors and students throughout our lives. So mentors may not always appear as we might think a mentor would; typically teaching via some kind of platform, whether classes, books, workshops or coaching. Mentors can teach us through living example whereby we can 'tune-in' to their particular frequency[16], which also means to entrain to their energy; different language, same meaning. Mentors show up and reflect aspects of ourselves back to us and perhaps abilities that we were not fully aware of or could trust in.

Biologically speaking, entrainment is the synchronisation of organisms to an external rhythm. It is to align an internal rhythm or energy to an external rhythm, which is something we all do all of the time, usually without realising it. A well-known example of entrainment is when women start living together and often find that their menstrual cycles begin to align in rhythm. One woman's inner rhythm will entrain to the strongest external rhythm, which may be her or the other woman.

In our modern world, the external rhythm in our big cities is fast and so when we entrain to this rhythm, we also need to learn to entrain to a slower one and to find our own natural rhythm so that we don't burn out. We can dance the rhythms, knowing when to speed up and when to slow down much like the flow between masculine and feminine ways of being.

---

[16] Read more on frequency in chapter 13, Nature.

THE ILLUSION OF SEPARATION

SEPARATION

I feel sea all around today.
I know
because I'm panicking:
uncontrollable sobbing,

not crying, but sobbing —
there's a difference.

Lying on the grass outside,
trying to breathe,
but I've become an island today.
There is no causeway,
no boat to reach me
from the other side.

Is that why I'm sobbing
making strange sounds?

I read a few lines from a novel,
the words are like tethers
tying me to Earth,
to the real.

Words become a salve
helping me breathe,
calming me.

It's as if I were a child,

a baby,

with red, puffy, teary eyes;

a child that needs to feel tied,

to a loving someone,

a human touch

reminding her where she is,

bringing her back to the here and now.

I close the book.

Waves rise up to overwhelm again;

music, put on some music-

ah, the soothing words,

a melody,

stories being sung to me,

Bic Runga,

reminding me where I've been.

I sing along, go online,

and tip-tap my feelings to someone

who has been on this island.[17]

—*Jane Alexandra Cormack*

The above poem captures a moment of separation. The felt experience of disconnection from the world and all that is in it. Disconnect can happen when we feel we are alone in the world and can emerge alongside depression, low self-esteem and unclarity about who we really are. We think that there is no-one else on Earth that gets what it feels like when we

---

[17] Jane Alexandra Cormack, 2008.

are in that place. That of course, is completely untrue.

None of us can ever be truly disconnected from everything on Earth because this is where we are. We are connected simply by being here. **It is our thoughts that disconnect us from life.** It is when we isolate ourselves believing that no-one really understands, when we might not know or forget how to feel and love, that we think we are disconnected. Humans *want* to feel love and connection. Love is all that we want because love is the way we connect. Love is all that we are. As babies, we were completely dependent on our caregivers who had to 'care' enough to allow us to survive. To connect to love is to feel the warmth of life, the living energy of another person, animal or plant.

There are many ways for us to separate from each other. We become separated into groups, organisations, cultures, race, and religion and in many other smaller ways. These groups have their place and do serve humanity by creating focus on certain ideas and structures. Gathering in groups of like-minded people can support us on our journey. It can help us to feel that we are not alone in our unique way of thinking or doing things. We want to be with our soul family and our tribe to feel a sense that we belong and to feel safe. It is still separation. It can be easy to become entrenched and trapped in our own bubbles, which can make it harder to go out into the world and connect with new people we don't usually identify with. We find balance by walking into and through other, different kinds of bubbles[18] than those we have become used to because we experience different aspects of our personalities when we come into contact with new people, cultures or situations. It is important to always stay interested and curious about life and be open to new possibilities.

The Language of the World expressed itself *through me* in the above poem. I became the language by writing to myself. My resolution was to

---

[18] Read chapter 12 on Purpose for more on bubbles.

read the words of a book, which helped to tether and connect me to the Earth—to write the poem, to listen to music and feel the familiarity of singer Bic Runga's words, whom I saw in concert in New Zealand. And I began to type out these feelings and sent them to a friend whom I knew would understand what it felt like to be in that place. I was able to do things that I knew would help to reconnect me to humanity and create a causeway from the island I had placed myself on.

The next time you become aware of feeling disconnected, isolated or alone, allow yourself to feel that, there is always wisdom in our pain. Then do something that will help to reconnect you tangibly with the world around you. This could be a few very simple things, like going for a walk in nature and being very alert to your surroundings. Becoming present in this moment immediately reconnects you to your current reality. Call or write to a friend whom you know will 'get' you, listen to some music you love or read an inspiring magazine or book, dance and feel your own body moving again, marvel at the starry sky or the colour of the autumn leaves. Doing any of these things will help you feel grounded on the Earth and reconnected with humanity.

LIFE-CHANGING RELATIONSHIPS

It is through our relationships with each other that we can learn, deepen and grow the most. We often travel more deeply within intimate, romantic relationships because we are fully connected energetically, emotionally, spiritually, mentally and physically. The most impactful relationships challenge us to open our hearts beyond what we are capable of doing alone. We can experience joy, sensual pleasure, love, intimacy and deep connection yet when our longing is unmet we can also experience anger, hurt and dissatisfaction; the whole range of the emotional spectrum is opened up through relationship. Breathtaking experiences in nature can open our hearts, but there is nothing like a human-to-human connection to expand and open us.

Life changing relationships show us how much we are capable of loving. Many people experience the relationship with a beloved pet changes their life, because animals can unconditionally love us and open our hearts where they might be closed in romantic relationships.

Although 'following your heart' can mean following connections with the people who you feel a spark with, attraction is not always about sexual attraction. It can simply be an attraction to someone you resonate or are in alignment with for all manner of reasons. You may be attracted to a fellow messenger who appears for a short moment in your life to share something with you. It's important to follow up on these connections to see what might unfold.

We create impact in other people's lives when we touch the golden threads of truth within them that lead to the light of who they are.

The *Love and Relationships* Pleasure Project

Take out your Pleasure Project journal and find a quiet spot to do this exercise or create a collage filled with photographs and words.

MESSENGERS

Mentally travel back over your life so far and begin to write down the names of people or animals who created an impact in your life. These could be people or a pet that supported you when you needed it most. It may be someone who showed up at just the right moment when you couldn't see any other solution to your situation or someone who inspired you by example, to completely change the direction of your life.

1. **Was there someone who completely opened up your world to a new experience of life? Who?**

2. **What did they share or show you that catalysed this change?**

3. **Perhaps there was someone whose guidance you followed only to discover you didn't want what they showed you? (Write their names here).**

4. How did this experience benefit you?

5. What did they teach you?

6. Who is currently in your life that you consider yourself to have a 'challenging' relationship with?

7. What do you find challenging about the relationship?

8. What is this teaching you about yourself? What are you learning from your interactions with this person/s?

SEEING MAGNIFICENCE

9. Which relationships do you cherish in your life?

10. What is it about those relationships that you cherish the most? How do you feel in the presence of those people?

Practice seeing the magnificence in everyone you meet. Especially those people who upset or annoy you the most. Observe the judgements (without judging yourself) that pop into your mind when you spend time with people. This takes practice because we do it all the time, often without noticing. When we practice seeing the magnificence in someone else, they feel it, just as you would feel it. Watch them change as you do.

Chapter Summary

- Who you choose to spend time with is important
- Every person that enters your life is a messenger bringing exactly what you need in that moment
- The most important relationship you have in your life is with yourself
- You are born with worth and leave the planet with it intact
- You show others how to treat you by the example of how you treat yourself
- You 'entrain' to the people you spend time with
- Complete disconnection from life is impossible; if you are still alive, you are connected in some way, therefore, to be completely separate and alone is an illusion
- Relationships are life changing

CHAPTER SIX

The Language of
Giving and Receiving

We breathe in, we breathe out. From the moment we inhale our first breath on leaving the womb and entering this world, until the last outward breath leaves our body when we depart; the natural cycle of breathing does not fully complete until then. Its rhythm and motion continue to flow in cycles within our bodies, sustaining this life. There is a give and take of life from birth to death. We cannot give our breath *out*, before we have received our breath *in*.

If we look at the art of giving and receiving purely from the standpoint of procreation, then we recognise that a woman's body is designed to receive; the sperm seed is received and fertilises an egg to gestate, grow, evolve and then she can birth her new child.

We can apply this to anything we want to 'birth' or give. So we cannot give, unless there is something to give *from*, unless the seeds of ideas have been received and planted. We cannot give birth from emptiness. The seed must be planted and given time to grow. Or as the saying goes, 'We cannot give water from a dry well'. There's nothing to give and if we do try to give from the emptiness, we start to corrode ourselves from the inside. Just as the dry well gets drier and drier and starts to crack.

There is an art to both giving and receiving. Giving and receiving are in fact the same thing. It's the circular motion of energy that moves through you to both give and receive. When you receive, you are also giving to yourself by saying yes to the giving *and* giving of your joy when you receive with an open heart. And when you give to another, you are also receiving for yourself; what you receive is the joy, satisfaction or love of giving when you contribute to someone else's happiness. Yet people often find themselves 'stuck' in one place or the other. Giving and giving and feeling depleted without fully receiving. Or receiving and hoarding, without giving back. I call giving and receiving an 'art' because it is an art to know and trust when enough actually is enough and when you are limiting and not allowing yourself to receive what you asked for because you don't feel 'worthy' or 'good enough'. The 'art' part comes in recognising that there is a natural flow. There will be times in our lives when we appear to receive more and times when we appear to give more. The art is to enjoy each phase as it comes, knowing there will always be future opportunities to give and receive.

What has giving and receiving got to do with the Language of the World, you may wonder? Well, you receive guidance and messages all the time as well as 'give' them to yourself and other people. You are a messenger. For you to be able to receive, see and feel this guiding language, you need to open to it.

RECEIVING IS SELFISH?

DIVA[19]

Corroborate my stories,
consolidate my love,
tell me I'm a genius,

---

[19] Jane Alexandra Cormack, 2003.

that light shines on me from above.
Give me all or nothing,
serve my every whim,
believe in me, trust in me,
make me a perfect gin.
Understand my feelings,
inside and out,
tell everyone I'm wonderful,
that you can't help but shout it out.
Validate my existence,
fulfil all my desires,
be my puppet on a string,
allow me to control your wires.
Agree with everything I say,
pretend you understand,
when I emerge to the world outside,
be there to take my hand.
Massage my ego if I'm feeling low,
make me a Turkish bath,
follow me and be there wherever I go,
clean up the aftermath.
Worship the ground I walk upon,
surround me with beautiful flowers,
lavish me with attention and expensive gifts,
succumb to my seductive powers.
Be my alias, my alibi,
handle my confrontations,
take care of my expenses
and NEVER test my patience.

—*Jane Alexandra Cormack*

Many of us were taught that there's a limit to how much we should allow ourselves to have or experience and so we believe that receiving is selfish or self-centred. There is still a deep underlying guilt and fear of appearing selfish if we take too much. To be labelled a 'Diva', like the woman in the poem above, would be horrifying for so many women. We label these types of women 'demanding' and judge them for their apparent self-centred nature.

Then the custom can be to over-give from the 'need' of not wanting to appear selfish. So then are we really giving? Rather than giving from the overflowing joy and true desire to share and give, we give from feeling obligated to do so. What is in the giving if it arises from a place of lack or unworthiness within?

When you do something that feels good for you, it feels good for the whole because your joy in receiving is contagious and uplifting to others. So it may appear that you receive more than another person, yet in allowing yourself to receive, you are also automatically giving. The flow of energy continues and like a fully charged battery, you have the energy to be the 'charge' in others' lives.

We give to ourselves by choosing to receive. So giving to self is also receiving *for* self and as mentioned above, is the same energy. Humans try to separate everything to make sense of it but this often causes further confusion as we do not see the 'wholeness' of the cycle and with all natural rhythms, there is a cycle.

In chapter 2, The Forgotten Language of Pleasure, we discussed the relationship between pleasure and guilt and of the moment of choice in which we can enjoy the satiation of the pleasures we love and have received or to stretch beyond what may feel good due to compulsions, addictions or the need to numb or suppress feelings. So there is a fine balance in allowing ourselves to receive through giving to ourselves. When we topple across that fine line, we fall into self-destructive behaviour.

The Key to find is this: take as much as you need to feel satiated and no more and always give back in kind. I love the movie, 'Pay it Forward'.[20] Rather than pay back what we receive from the same person, the movie calls us to trust that there will always be a future opportunity to give back in ways that are fitting and delight us.

GIVING

There are so many ways in which we already give that do not arise from a place of forcefulness or obligation or that need involve money.

In my Feminine Focus classes and workshops, I guide women to expand their radiance and allow themselves to be seen whilst looking into the eyes of their partner. This can often feel a bit scary to some, but we focus on the power of the practice. During one class, I acted as 'partner' for a participant. As my partner opened energetically, I sat within the field of her energetic radiance and tears came to my eyes. I saw and felt her expanding energy field fill the room like a radiant light moving from dim to full power and simultaneously felt my heart open and expand. I was honoured that she felt safe in my presence to show her vulnerable, exquisitely beautiful light. It was truly a gift for me to receive and I was uplifted and full of joy for the rest of the day having witnessed and been present with her.

---

[20] *Pay it Forward*. Dir. Mimi Leder, (USA, 2000, Warner Brothers Pictures).

Allowing yourself to be fully seen is a gift for other people because your energy can touch and uplift them in ways you could never imagine.

Below is a list of ways that you may already give so much but not realise it. In the column on the right, or in your Pleasure Project journal, you can continue the list of all the ways that you personally and uniquely give to the world.

Ways You May Already Give without Knowing It >>	Other Ways I Give >>
<ul><li>You give of your presence</li><li>You give of your essence and your energy</li><li>Your feminine radiance</li><li>You give of your example; you can be a catalyst for change for others</li><li>You give of your inspiration and ideas</li><li>You give emotional support</li><li>You give physical support</li><li>You give a smile</li><li>You give a kiss</li><li>You give a kick up the ass</li><li>You give insights</li><li>You give of your truth</li><li>You give your companionship</li><li>You give your love</li></ul>	

THE OVER-GIVER

How much is too much? When you give all of yourself away, you may think you are being 'selfless', yet if you feel depleted energetically, emotionally, mentally or otherwise then you're over-giving and not receiving enough. As hard as it can be sometimes, it is our own responsibility to say "No" and to start giving to ourselves by allowing others to give to us.

A lot of women over-give and try to be 'people-pleasers'. Not wanting to hurt others, let them down, break a promise or to be seen to be—SELF-ISH. This is often to the detriment of their own wellbeing and dishonors themselves. We *know* when we have not honoured ourselves and have stretched that little bit too far. An 'over-giver' who doesn't replenish the water in her giving well, is going to dry out pretty fast. Plumped with pleasure, she is not.

Selflessness has been put on a pedestal and worshipped giving women an unhealthy, unrealistic mode of transport into their bodily and energetic demise. The equivalent of the raisin in chapter 2, "Pleasure forgotten, raisins scatter the ground".[21] A selfless act can be described as giving without the concern of self but only for the needs and wishes of others. This can be a beautiful experience and love calls the way, we give because we love to, because we care, because we love *love*, because we *are* love. We give because it makes us feel good and because we want others to feel good too. But over-giving can be an addictive pattern like any other and a way to ignore the souls voice crying from within to listen, to rest, to recharge, to receive.

To give unconditionally is to give without expectation of return. And yet the return always shows up at some point in wonderful, unexpected ways. Often we are called to give without a second thought, for example,

---

[21] From chapter 2, The Forgotten Language of Pleasure.

when someone falls over in the street, our natural impulse leads us to run over and help them. We don't spend time thinking about it. I have received so much from people who were strangers while on my travels, who helped me when I needed it most. It's not that we need to wait to receive a great fortune before giving, we don't. Some people, who have very little materially, give the most. It's the quality and energy behind the giving that matters. To be fully present with yourself as you give to another means you are less likely to give in a way that leaves you feeling depleted.

QUALITY OF GIVING

The old adage 'It's quality, not quantity' applies here, so over-givers, listen in! There is quality or not in our giving. Other people can sense if what we give comes from a place of fullness or from lack. From joy or obligation.

When we give from lack or unworthiness, we may find what we give is not accepted by the other person and thus, *we feel* rejected. This may often be because we give from the need to give and not from sensing what is required or wished for. There is a lack of consciousness in giving what is really needed because the only 'need' present, is the need to give to try and feel better.

In not allowing ourselves to receive and not giving to ourselves as well, then the quality of what we try to give to others diminishes in terms of giving of our love, energy and source. It is not as nourishing to receive the last dirty dregs of water from the drying well than it is from the well that's filled with clean water. There are plenty of resources for us all to give from a full well and to receive a multitude of gifts in many forms.

HOW TO PRACTICE LETTING LOVE IN

How many times has someone commented on your lovely new dress and your instant reply has been, "Oh this, I got this for £2 in a charity shop?" Did you let the compliment in? No, you didn't, you threw it right back. So then the giver feels like his or her 'gift' of a compliment was rejected. You are giving a gift someone just gave you right back to them and saying, "I don't like it, take it back". Ouch!

Letting in compliments can be very uplifting and incredibly nourishing for women. They may also feel a little uncomfortable to let in if you are not accustomed to attention, but if you do, they can have a similar effect to water feeding a flower, which begins to open and blossom. If the compliment is healthy, i.e. genuine and loving and we let it in, by feeling it, it can actually influence and change our energetic state of being. Given that our universe is composed of energy, we are affected by and can affect the energetic vibration of each other.[22] Certain 'frequencies' or waves of energy have a higher or lower vibration which, in terms of emotions, we often define as positive or negative because they feel different. That is not to say that feeling sadness or anger is wrong or bad. They are natural human emotions that need to be acknowledged and felt. However, the sense of feeling lighter or uplifted when we feel good is no coincidence. As the energy of love is measured as a high vibration, when we allow in a loving compliment, we usually feel good, lighter and appreciated. We literally have allowed ourselves to be 'uplifted' vibrationally by letting love in. When we are uplifted in this way, we naturally allow in more abundance in all ways because we are more open to it and have more awareness of it when it shows up.

---

[22] If you would like to learn the science behind the points I mention here on energy and vibration, then I suggest delving into the ever evolving and vast field of Quantum Physics and Theory.

When offering a compliment to someone else, wait. Wait until a thought or feeling bubbles up from deep within you, from a place of fullness within. Wait until *you* feel it first. And then, give it like a gift that you feel delighted to give. Do not try to force out a compliment or words, the recipient will feel that it's not genuine or authentic.

To get the flow of energy moving, you can begin with some obvious appreciations of a woman's physical beauty or her choice in creative style, i.e., the combination of colours, clothing and jewellery she has put together. Once you begin to see and feel this woman on the outside, you can begin to tune-in to deeper aspects of her personality, her presence, her energy and any gifts or skills you may notice she possesses.

And likewise as you begin to *give* your gifts of compliments to the woman, she *receives* them and begins to open and show more of herself, and then *you* feel and see more of her and feel uplifted as you *receive*. So both women give and receive. She is radiating because she is being fully seen by you and feels safe to show more of who she is. She, in turn, gives back to you as you bask in her radiance and feel uplifted. Which, believe me, is a true gift. **To bask in the radiance of an open women is to feel *your* heart open, is to be uplifted, is to have your defences melted, is to feel her magnificence and thus, the reflection of your own magnificent and radiant goddess nature. This is good.**

The foundation of any genuine compliment is LOVE. Love is the foundation for everything and is where we all return to. We are acting in love and giving love. So if you deflect a genuine and healthy compliment, you are also deflecting receiving love.

There needs to be 'settling time' in order to fully receive. This means that when you receive a compliment, that you pause and let it 'settle' within you before responding with thanks. The compliment is love in the form of energy that tangibly and physically enters your energetic field. If you allow yourself to fully receive it and feel it, your body will soften, your heart will begin to open, you will feel 'fed' and 'seen' and open further in trust showing more of your radiance. This is a fantastic Pleasure Project that you can practice with your friends, simple and free!

THE GIVING UNIVERSE

In chapter 5, Love and Relationships, I wrote about the prevalence of the 'not good enough' syndrome in our culture. Our world within is reflected in our world without and our belief systems create the views that we see. So, as we think specific thoughts about ourselves, such as not being good enough, we emit the vibration of this thought which communicates to the world that we don't deserve what we want. You may have a deep desire for something, such as an intimate loving relationship, close friendships, new red shoes or to make a positive difference in the world. That desire draws the experience, object or opportunity into your reality, which very often, looks different than you may have imagined and as a result, you're more inclined to dismiss what shows up. But if you also don't feel you are good, deserving or ready enough to receive it, you won't. You will find a way to deflect the gift. And you will continue to receive what you DO feel you deserve until you feel you deserve or simply want something more or different.

Our wants and desires are always limited by what we feel we deserve, as well as what we believe to be possible. Yet we still need to take the first step after recognising the sensation of the first want because it's only by saying 'yes' to this sense of wanting that we will know whether we actually want it or not.

THE WAYS WE DEFLECT RECEIVING

There are many subtle ways that we can deflect receiving. And it's often not until someone else points it out that we even realise what we're doing.

Do you block or resist receiving in any of these ways?
- Saying thank you too quickly
- Laughing in response to a compliment someone gives you
- Trying to 'pull out' another compliment by putting yourself down, although you haven't allowed the first one to settle yet
- 'Closing' your body by crossing your arms and legs or hiding behind your hair
- Diverting attention to someone else
- Changing the subject
- Returning the compliment or offer of help/support very quickly
- Having to 'suddenly' leave
- Allowing yourself to be distracted by your phone/texting
- Avoiding eye contact
- Pretending you didn't hear what the person said to you
- Humour—cracking a joke to 'break' the energy coming your way so you don't have to receive it
- Trying to be in control in all of the above examples

The next time someone gives you a compliment or offers you help and support, notice if you let yourself bask in it or respond in one or more ways from the above list. Notice what you may resist receiving, from whom and what it feels like. When we want to make new changes in our lives, this is where we often meet resistance, so it's important to be aware of the emotions that arise in this place of resistance.

ABUNDANCE

Abundance, like everything else in life, is something we need to be open to receive. Abundance includes the receiving of everything that life has to offer. Money, jobs, relationships, travel, a new dress, dinner from a friend, a cup of coffee from a stranger, a compliment, a gift, an uplifting hug from a child, comfort from your dog, the offer of a massage, help to build a website or fix your car or simply feeling rich in the presence of nature. These are all forms of abundance. They are all ways of letting life in. But you can only let life and abundance in if you think you are worthy of it. If you think you deserve it. 'YES! I damn well deserve it all!!' says your mind, but deeper inside you, something continues to say 'NO'. The fears, worry or sense of low self-esteem that you feel is expressed through the energy that you emit and can prevent you from fully seeing, embracing and accepting what arrives in your reality.

Your ability to give and receive abundance is related to the holding in or giving out of your gifts; your knowledge, in whatever format that arrives, as well as your compassion, generosity and love. If we allow ourselves to receive by developing a compassionate, loving and healthy relationship with ourselves, like a fountain, we can overflow that abundance back into the world, yet are always full. We get into the feminine flow and natural cycles of giving and receiving with a full heart.

MONEY IS LIKE HONEY

Money is sweet and fluid like honey, or it can be. And like everything else in this world, it is a tool for us to use. Money has so many stigmas around it although it is no different from any other form of energetic exchange. Most of us have *negative* stigmas and associations around money, which have been unconsciously taught to us by parents and society. These associations develop into the deeply ingrained belief systems we hold. So often this can make money appear to be more difficult to receive or let in, than the offer of a nice dinner from a friend. Both are forms of receiving abundance, but one form, for so many people, is easier to receive than the other.[23]

A life chasing money alone can be pretty lonely and empty. But money is wonderful. The pieces of paper and small circles of metal represent an exchange of energy. We are always exchanging energy and money plays just one small part in this exchange. We exchange the same energy that money represents in different ways every day. We offer help, our services and feel good giving gifts that are joyfully received as well as receiving special, thoughtful gifts from others. We swap an apple for a pear with a friend rather than an apple for a coin, which may later be exchanged for a pear.

Again, abundance relates to value. We exchange value for value. If we believe an apple is more valuable than a pear, we may want two pears to compensate for the value of one apple. It is an agreement and an exchange that feels both good and reasonable. Do you believe your gifts and talents give value? If so, are you receiving value in exchange for them? The bottom line is, you will *know* if you've been paid accordingly for what you provided because it will feel right, good and balanced for both of you. But sometimes this value comes in indirect ways:

You might hold a workshop and have put an incredible amount of energy and preparation into its design. But only two people show up. You hold the planned workshop anyway and give all the content you would have given for twenty people, to two. Those two people receive a lot from you. And

---

[23] Read more on abundance in chapter 12, Purpose.

you learn a thing or two from them. But because you had to cover your costs, venue, etc., you make a financial loss. Yet the universe has recognised the value you have given and you also feel that you gave your best, but really would have liked to make a profit from all that you provided. The following day, you check your e-mails in the afternoon and find that your e-book and several pieces of jewellery from your online store have been sold! Plus there's an e-mail from one of the participants asking you if you will hold a private workshop for several of her friends because she learnt so much from your workshop and wants to share it.

Value given, value received. Just not in the way you may expect. We have placed so many restrictions and fear around money, but if we learn to love it, look at our individual beliefs and where they stem from that may have us 'stuck' and see it for what it is, a tool; then we can begin to loosen constriction a little, even a lot, so that our 'set' honey money pot begins to melt, allowing money to flow like runny honey.

The *Giving and Receiving* Pleasure Project

1. **Do you regularly give more than you feel you have in you and/or more than you receive?**

2. **How do you feel when you over-give?**

If you regularly over-give, ask a friend to practice giving you some compliments and notice if they feel easy or challenging for you to let in.

3. **Do you hold back from sharing your gifts, your voice, thoughts, ideas or opinions?**

4. **How do you feel when you hold back?**

If you hold back, notice when a compliment pops into your head when you are around your friends and rather than hold it in your mind, give the gift to her/him and speak it; notice what changes may appear in your friend and how she/he relates to you afterwards.

5. **What forms of abundance are present for you right now?**
Hint: Ideas and visions are forms of abundance because they lead you to it.

6. In how many ways have you received today?

Examples:

- Appreciations and compliments
- A car ride to the train station
- A friendly, comfortable place to stay for the night
- A foot rub
- Love from your dog
- The sun warming your back

7. How did it feel to receive these things?

8. What do you want to receive now? Be honest with yourself and aware of your own belief systems about what you really feel is possible for you to receive right now. For example, suddenly exclaiming, "Yes I want to receive £1 million!" while simultaneously having an inner belief that it's not possible for you, is likely going to leave you feeling disappointed. Start simply and go deeper into what would genuinely feel good. If that happens to be some extra finances, then feel into what you want it for and how it would feel to receive that. And be gentle with yourself while having fun doing this project, it can take time to learn how to open and allow in more.

Examples:

- Deeper intimacy with my partner
- To feel appreciated
- Extra finances
- More adventure
- A massage
- A hug
- More time to relax
- Support to look after my children
- Help around the house
- Technical assistance with my online business

9. How would it feel to receive what you want to receive now?
Visualise what you would like being given to you and imagine how it feels. Inwardly claim what would feel joyful to receive and notice any judgements that may arise around deserving it.

Stay open to how and when what you want, shows up in your life. For example, if your desire is to experience deeper intimacy with your partner, then that might arrive as a friend lending you a tantra CD, meeting a couples coach whom you like at an event, simply having a conversation with your partner to express your wishes or you deciding to take inspired action and arrange an intimate or special evening together.

May these practices support you in opening to the abundance waiting for you in all ways.

Chapter Summary

- Think about the quality, rather than quantity of how and what you give
- Practice giving and receiving compliments with your friends and notice how you feel
- Notice in which life areas, you don't feel 'good enough' to receive
- Notice where and how you deflect receiving and practice receptivity where it feels good, yet where you still resist it
- Giving and receiving is like breathing in and out
- It's very healthy to allow yourself to receive, as well as to give; it is the natural cycle mirrored in nature
- Receiving is NOT selfish and you won't look like a 'Diva'!
- You already give in so many ways
- The Key: take as much as you need to feel satiated and no more and always give back in kind

CHAPTER SEVEN

The Language of Home and Sanctuary

Modern life brings a multitude of lifestyle choices. Many people are born in one country, brought up in another, or move to work in different parts of the world. You may have been rooted in the same place your whole life but all your friends have moved away. You may have parents from two different cultures who live somewhere in-between or perhaps you are a modern day nomad who moves countries every few years. All of these experiences can bring up questions around home and belonging. Where do you feel at home? Where do you belong? Are you at home in your body, at home in your country or with who you are? Home has so many meanings.

We can feel 'at home' with some people and not with others, we can feel at home in our space or feel uncomfortable in it. Home can mean your country of birth, or it could be where you live now or lived last year. We have our geographical home, the home or homes we spent our childhood in and our own family home. You may live in your home but still harbour a longing to feel that you truly belong somewhere. At home with your tribe, at home with your family or lover, at home wherever you happen to be and even at home on the planet.

Where and what is home to you?

YOUR INNER AND OUTER HOME

Our first sense of home is being in our mothers' womb. Safe, warm and held within a liquid cocoon. Then, an experience of warm familiarity and cradling in the arms of your mother or primary caregiver may have led to feeling home as a child. When we are born, our own bodies become our homes. They become our real sanctuaries, if we make them so. Yet as we grow and for a multitude of reasons, so many humans begin to abuse the sanctity and sanctuary of their bodies. Overeating, extreme exercise, self-starvation, no exercise, junk food, drugs, alcohol, overwork and exhaustion. There are many ways to abuse the sanctuary of the body, your home. And when the body is tired, overweight, underweight, has not seen the light of day for weeks or is filled with toxic substances, there can be a lot of resistance to actually wanting to return 'home' to the body. It can feel incredibly uncomfortable to be in a body that has an almost uninhabitable environment and can leave you feeling completely disconnected from it—drowning out her true voice and language.

Imagine creating the feeling of being in a home that you'd actually love to 'come home' to. A happy, warm, clean, safe place to be that is filled with your own unique expression and energy. Imagine nourishing your inner environment so your 'home' works efficiently and smoothly, so that it's fresh and cleansed because you are happy to be there taking care of it. You feed, exercise and nourish your body with pure food and water. You rest it each night and wake up in the morning feeling refreshed and excited for the unfolding of a new day. You recognise the sacred nature of your body and home and treat it as such, so that you can listen to her language and experience more pleasure through her.

This feeling of being happy in the inner home environment of your body can extend outward to include your outer home environment. The way you treat and care for your body is often reflected in your outer environment as well. In times of chaos and internal confusion, it's all too easy to let self-care slide when in fact this is when your level of self-care needs to be 'upped'. When our inner environment is chaotic, it can often lead to a chaotic outer environment.

Are you currently happy in the home you live in? Do you take care of your outer home as you do your body? Do you give your body an environment in which it can thrive, feel safe, let go and be inspired?

PHYSICAL FOUNDATIONS

Your home and sanctuary are your physical foundations while you're on the planet. Your home may change many times during your life. Or you may be rooted in one place on Earth for your entire lifetime. If you're someone like me who loves to travel and has moved around a lot, then you'll have the experience of living in many different kinds of environments. This can be pretty useful in honing in on the kind of environments you thrive best in. You learn what you need, so that you can feel 'at home' and happy in the place you are.

At different stages of our lives, we may need a change of environment. When children leave home, or you separate from your partner, or your work leads you to a new country, or you've just had enough of the wet, grey weather! We seek out new beginnings and a new home to support our new desires and circumstances. We seek a place that is fertile in supporting our current path and purpose in life. A place that is fertile to receive who we are and what we bring. We can also feel guided to places where we experience deeply challenging periods of growth and are stretched in unexpected ways. The Language of the World and the feminine can guide our way to the home that is most suited for us at each stage of the journey, through repetitive messages that can arrive via messengers, word, symbol, colour, music, numbers, images, a vision or dream, or just a very clear sense of direction.

At some point, we may even find ourselves without an external home, or between homes:

In 2006-2007, I lived in New Zealand, the first year in the South island and in the second year I moved to the North Island. In the south, I'd been living in the most beautiful, grand pink house, with a balcony overlooking a breathtaking view of the Remarkables Mountains and Lake Wakatipu. It really was remarkable. But new work opportunities were calling me north and although I wasn't sure where I was going to live, even a couple of weeks before my scheduled leaving time, I had the feeling I wanted to be around lots of youthful people like me. I started on my road trip north through New Zealand with a friend, still not having arranged anywhere to live. Two weeks later, we arrived in Auckland and I said farewell to my friend who was doing a round the world trip. I booked myself into a lovely youth hostel, which was just like one of the local houses, and ended up living there for six weeks. It was such a contrast to where I had been living before but I made so many great friends and my social and home life was so much fun. Then, through a friend I had made while living in Australia, an opportunity arose to house-sit in a gorgeous little cottage in the lush rainforests near Auckland. After sharing space with so many people in the hostel, which I had loved at the time, I was ready for my own space again where I could relax, enjoy my own company and focus on my work.

Ultimately, the Earth is our home, the body is our home, home is where the heart is and the heart may be drawn to many different places to call home.

ISOLATION AND DISCONNECTION

Homes can also be isolating, a place to hide, to disconnect from life and wallow in loneliness. A small flat in a large city can feel like a cosy sanctuary to some people or an empty, cold prison to others. The evolution towards single unit families today from our ancestor's communities and tribes has contributed to a sense of disconnection currently familiar to so many people.

Still, there are many people without a physical home; the streets are their home or a homeless shelter. Some people choose to live without a steady home or to live deep in nature, outside, close to the elements. It is the energy of love that infuses a home or 'place' with fullness, with life and the feeling of being alive. The energy of love is what creates a true home, whether that home is made of mud, is up a tree in a forest in Russia, whether it's a castle on a hill in Scotland, an open plan apartment in New York City, in the favelas of Rio De Janeiro, in a lighthouse on the most northern tip of Norway or in a caravan that traverses the globe. **If your home is filled with the energy of love and with your expression of love, then it is truly home.**

BELONGING AND COMMUNITY

Humans thrive when we feel a sense of belonging and this is what we search for. To meet a soul mate, to find our tribe, to connect with people like us, for family and roots and for some kind of solid foundation in which to feel safe, seen, loved, acknowledged for who we are and what gifts we can contribute.[24] We experience contrast as well as commonalities in the company of others. It is through spending time with people that our own valuable skills and gifts, we may have taken for granted, are often discovered or revealed.

We all need some time and space to be with ourselves, some more than others. Yet, we also need the love, support, diversity and joy that comes in connection with communities of friends and family who share similar values.

So what does community mean and look like to you?

The feminine element within us yearns for connection and a sense of community. But with our individualistic way of modern living, for many, this yearning is not being met. We can, however, create community wherever we go. Sacred women's circles and groups offer a strong foundation for creating sisterhood and help connect us with the missing element that we search for; new friends and deep connection with ourselves and others, support, collaboration and the bonds of community or 'family'. Our neighbours and friends in our village or city can be our local community if we make an effort to reach out and connect. And we are, of course, a global community that can connect and communicate within groups online. Any kind of 'bubble' or group is a community of people who circle around a common theme. This is the foundation for Intentional communities that are established from the outset with a clear and common vision and lifestyle. This could be a spiritual vision, political, social or religious group like an ecovillage or a student co-operative. Intentional and ecovillage communities are popping up all over the world as more and more people feel drawn back to this way of life.

---

[24] In chapter 11, Purpose, I talk about the different 'bubbles' we belong to.

Back in my Grandparent's era, family communities were tight, partly because families were much larger. My Paternal Grandfather was the eldest of eight siblings and my Maternal Grandmother the eldest of five and there were many cousins, aunties and uncles too. These large family communities where the wider family took care of each other and children learned from elders while having plenty of other children to play with, were more common. Now women bear fewer children, particularly in the west and families are dispersed around the globe.

HOME OR SANCTUARY?

Rather than a place to dump and store your stuff, to sleep, eat and be a shelter from the rain, make your home a sanctuary. When people deliberately choose to enter into a sanctuary space, they go to regenerate their energy. They go to be in stillness, to let go, to listen, to feel who they are, to cleanse and clear their emotional, mental and physical energy. A sanctuary is a haven to re-energise, to return to yourself, to completely relax and to get clarity. It is a place of safety. Imagine that your home, whether house, flat, caravan or castle, is this sanctuary. Whether you live alone, live with your family or extended family, friends or housemates; it's possible to create a sanctuary space for yourself and for those you live with.

You can have your own private sanctuary space within your home if you share it, as well as infuse your loving care and attention in the entire space for others to enjoy and feel 'home'. Even if you only live for a month or two in your home, you can create a place of beauty, light, colour and love.

CLEARING AND CLEANSING

Over time, your home may become filled with clutter, especially if you've lived there for years. You inherit things from your parents or grandparents, raise your children or leave an old career and, therefore, an old image behind. You can create sentimental attachments to objects, like the range of crystal decanters and glasses Granny left you, even though they are not 'you' and you don't particularly like them, you attach a memory to them. That memory ignites an emotional response in you that lets you 'travel' to a memory or several memories of your Granny.

The question is, do you want to be surrounded by objects that consistently ignite this emotional response in you and that 'travel' you back to a different place in time? If these memories are joyful and uplifting, they make you smile or remind you to be courageous or free, then allow them in your space. But if you hold them there because of a sense of obligation or guilt in 'giving away' the family jewels, then it's probably time to begin clearing your environment.

Cleansing and cleaning our physical home environment supports the flow of fresh, new energy to enter. It also supports clarity of mind. The spaciousness we create on the outside helps us to feel spaciousness within.[25] We want to create an optimal environment that supports who we want to be *now*. Not who we were five years or even six months ago. And for that, we require a clear space.

Letting go of the things that surround you can be difficult if you see them every day. This is why oftentimes when you return from a holiday or trip away, there's an urge to rid yourself of excess 'stuff'. The perspective change allows you to see more clearly what's meaningful and important to you. Travelling gives us the experience of feeling different aspects of

---

[25] Read chapter 12 on Freedom for more on this topic.

ourselves that have the space to emerge in these new environments. Our energy is 'shaken up' and we are reminded of feeling free. Freedom reminds us that it can feel better to be in a cleaner and a possibly more minimal environment.

Similarly, with clothing, you may find yourself clinging to items from certain eras in your life when you didn't feel good in your body, or pieces that were given to you by your ex-boyfriend. They may be perfectly good quality clothes, but you don't *feel* great when you wear them. They remind you of feeling frumpy or uncertain and doubtful of yourself. They remind you of a time when you tried to hide or please others in your appearance, when you didn't express the true language of who you are. These clothes can be passed onto a good home. It's time to free yourself of many material ties that don't represent who you want to be and where you want to go in your life.

Clean your space well with natural, chemical free products. Pure essential oils such as lemon oil are also naturally cleansing and leave a delicious, fresh smell in your home. You can add a few drops to your cleaning products. As you physically clean, you can simultaneously cleanse and clear out old, stagnant energy by intentionally filling every corner of your space with your loving presence. Remember chapter 2, The Forgotten Language of Pleasure, *"Where your attention and focus goes, your energy flows"*, well, this applies here too; giving attention to your home also flows positive energy into it. Give away objects and ornaments that no longer fill your heart with joy or connect you to the past and a memory of the 'you', that you no longer want to be.

Open the windows and let the wind of change blow through.

BEAUTY IN THE HOME

Beautiful environments are uplifting. They are physically beautiful, but it's also the energy within a home that creates the feeling of beauty; it's an atmosphere that is welcoming to a new visitor. You'll probably have had the experience of walking into an environment that feels uneasy and unwelcoming, it may even smell strange, feel 'cold' and generally feel uncomfortable to be in. Then there are places that seem so familiar, as if you've been there before and that you feel instantly at home and warm in and never want to leave!

Design, space, colour, texture, lighting, window views, art, plants and flowers, photographs, air quality and fragrance all create a home, just as you create yourself artistically through your style.[26] Your creativity and style, which is part of the 'language' of you, can also be expressed through your home. The way you arrange your furniture or your crockery is all part of your creative flair and as you put your energy into creating your space with art and plants and soft blankets and photographs that make you happy, you also infuse your space with the energy of love and care.

The feminine element within us revels in exterior beauty. Elements of nature brought into the home like plants and fresh flowers, crystals and stones bring the energy of nature inside. There should be no guilt or shame in *wanting* to be surrounded by beautiful things if they give you joy and uplift you.

Fill your space with beauty that you adore, because when you look around your home, you will feel joy. The space may include paintings you love; fabrics that feel soft and sensuous to the touch; sweet and spicy scents of essential oils, of cooking and fresh herbs; gifts given to you from your beloved and your friends; sea glass and pebbles collected from the

---

[26] See chapter 9 on Colour and Creating Yourself.

beach or gemstone jewels hanging from your mirror.

**All things in life are temporary, including your home.
So be in it fully, enjoy it fully and revel in your loving sanctuary.**

PLANET HOME

Our ultimate home is our beautiful planet Earth. Wherever we are on it, we are home. Nature is our home and every place we find ourselves in, we can call home. Like the turtle or the snail, you carry your home with you wherever you go. And, if you remember that you have the power to create potentials in friendships, work, love and magical opportunities anywhere, then you'll be at home no matter what village, town, city, community or country you find yourself in.

We all have an individual and collective relationship with the planet that we express through the actions we take. We show how we respect or disrespect nature, for example, whether we clean up after ourselves from a picnic or not. Just as mutual respect strengthens and supports our relationships with people, respect for the land and the planet strengthens our connection to her. We can show our respect by taking care of our planet through our daily choices. Recycling, reducing waste, using natural detergents for the home and for our personal use, sourcing natural fertilisers for the garden or growing and tending our own vegetable allotment helps us get back to the earth. *As I'm writing this chapter, Jason Mraz, a famous American singer songwriter's song, 'Back to the Earth', pops on my iPod! Check out the lyrics online!*

To feel immediately 'at home', go outside and place your bare feet on the soil. Walk around on soil (not concrete) for a while and you'll start to feel more grounded and connected to the Earth.

We are on the planet to enjoy her bounty, to marvel in and be inspired by her beauty, to create joyful, nourishing, loving lives together. She can be the provider of all that we need. Treat our Mother Earth as the sacred sanctuary home that she provides for us all.

The *Home and Sanctuary* Pleasure Project

1. Where do you feel the sense of being at home?

2. Who do you feel most 'at home' with of all the people you spend time with?

3. What is it about this person/people that makes you feel more or less 'at home'?

4. Are you living in a place (town, city, etc.) that supports you to thrive in your life? A place that you find inspiring, where you are stimulated or excited, filled with peace or challenged in a way that feels good when you walk out your front door?

5. Do you feel connected in your current home?

If the answer is no, try this short exercise to feel more comfortable with where you currently live:

FILLING YOUR SPACE WITH YOU

Go to a place in your home where you won't be disturbed. You can do this while standing up or sitting down, whatever feels more comfortable to you.

- Close your eyes and bring your awareness to your natural rhythm of breath and follow the flow of your breath as it moves through your body for a few moments

- Take a moment to tune-in to your physical body and notice how it feels

- Place your hands on your heart, now bring your awareness a few inches inside your body, behind your hands and feel your heart energy

- Visualise your heart as a glowing light that is opening and pulsing with your love; feel this light and love radiating outward with each breath you release

- See that light growing brighter and brighter in your heart with each inward breath you take and then see and feel the warmth and radiance of the light spreading outward and begin to fill the room with each outward breath you release

- See and allow that light to move outward beyond the room and fill your entire home with your energy and light

- Sense what that feels like for a few moments

- Bring your energy slowly back to your heart centre

- Return to feeling the rhythm of your natural breath, while being aware of how you feel

- When you feel ready and centred, open your eyes

You have just infused your home with you.

Questions to ask yourself >

Deeply feel into these questions and scribble 'quickly', in your Pleasure Project journal or here on this page, some answers and ideas that spring up.

6. **What kind of space will support me for what I want, who I want to be and what I want to do in my life right now?**

Do you need to live in a city where there are lots of opportunities to connect and try all kinds of new classes? Do you need the buzz of city life? Do you long for silence and nature? Or, do you feel you need to be closer to people you love? Is your deepest desire to live within a community of like-minded people? Do you want to be near a forest, in the mountains or by the ocean? Do you like to be warm or feel the four seasons come and go? Maybe you want to live between two countries or cities? Or experience living in many different countries?

Write the desires that are present for you just now.

7. **What kind of community do you want to have around you and how would you like to interact with them?**

8. **How do you want to feel in your home and why?** For example, 'I want to feel warm, so I can...'

If writing gives you pleasure then write on!

Or if visuals are your thing, which can be great for this particular project, check out Pinterest online and create a Home and Sanctuary board or get your hands dirty; get a huge piece of paper and create a collage, drawings or use photographs and home interior magazines for inspiration that speaks to your emotions.

LOVE + ROOF or SPACE = **HOME**

Chapter Summary

- Infuse your home with the essence of you
- Cleanse and clear your home with non-toxic products
- Create a foundation that feels good and that is a sanctuary for you and not just a place to dump your things
- Beautify your space, however small it may be, with things you love that uplift you when you see them
- Bring elements of nature inside
- Choose a place to live that provides the sense of community and belonging that you want to have and where you feel you will thrive
- Ask the universe to show you signs through the Language of the World to guide your way
- Respect and love your Planet Home

Part Three

CHAPTER EIGHT

The Language of Creative Self-Expression

When you express yourself creatively in the way that you love, the way that you get lost in for endless amounts of time, you are intently present. You keep returning to this form of creating, because it is your way of connecting to the divine within you. It returns you to 'you', to the most natural you. It is the way that you can touch on an endless universe inside that is both full and yet empty, waiting for your creations. It is the way that makes you both cry in surrender to what and whom you have always known you are, reach ecstatic, emotionally expansive heights and fettered lows. It is your love, your challenge, your pain and your passion.

And so you may avoid expressing yourself in the ways that you know light 'you' up because you are afraid of the power and depth of this vast and fathomless place within you. When you return there, you are both lost and found; lost, swimming within the infinite waters of your being, yet found within the expression and connection to your infinite self. You are connected to a reality beyond the one you currently see and your eyes are open wide; wider than the narrow slits you may usually see life through.

When you are faced and filled with the truth of who you are, you cannot avoid it.

The Language of the World speaks to you through the ways that light you up the most. Those 'ways' are often the foundations for your work and service in the world. Choosing those ways or tools carries your essence and expression forward, in the purest possible way.

THE POWER OF CREATIVE EXPRESSION

Sound, colour, movement, writing, drama and all expressive arts have been used as healing tools for centuries, although not always consciously. We creatively express ourselves in any kind of work that we do; creative expression is not solely for artists. So much creativity is expressed through technology now by writing blogs, filming and editing video, photography, graphics and so much more. However, it's important to balance creative online life with tactile creativity. Tactile creativity basically means using your hands and body to create with. It's 'hands on' creative expression that involves connecting physically with yourself and using your body as the tool. Cooking, making jewellery, painting, gardening, sculpture, pottery and dance are all forms of tactile creativity. These forms of creativity help ground you in your body and in turn lead you to be more present in the moment and not so focused 'in your head', as is often the result of excessively using technology.

THE LANGUAGE OF YOUR CREATIVE EXPRESSION

Creative expression is a powerful tool because it can be used as a doorway or portal into your source and is an outward expression of the life-force energy moving through you. The way you creatively express yourself is a language; it is *your* language and it is this outward expression that can bring you into a meditative state when you are in connection with the mysterious, universal flow; a higher frequency of energy that is your own divinity. Hidden parts of you can emerge via creative expression and this 'mirror' reveals aspects of yourself that you were not even aware of or did not want to look at. These parts of you can completely astound you.

DIVING IN

Her words,
sprayed onto paper,
are a liquid mirror
into which she delves,
bathes and drinks
to fill herself
with her energy
and dive into
depths
that love the self.[27]
—*Jane Alexandra Cormack*

It's important to find ways of expressing yourself that feel good, are joyful *and* that stretch your abilities and potential to the fullest. It may be just one way, such as becoming a film director or travel writer or it may be in numerous, individual or collective ways that combine various tools. There are many multi-passionate entrepreneurs in the world that are showing others a new way of bringing all their joys together to cre-

---

[27] Jane Alexandra Cormack, 2008.

ate a lifestyle that they love. The forms with which you choose to express yourself are just tools, they are vehicles for your expression. So choose some tools you love.

CREATIVE INSPIRERS

The creators that you admire are people who speak a similar language of expression as you. Knowing who creatively inspires you is to know your creative lineage and find a tribe that you feel you can 'belong' to. This can be an important exercise to recognise who you are becoming. When you begin to express yourself and share your voice through whatever medium you like, your tribe finds you. And you honour the tribe through the continuation, in your own very unique way, of the ancient creative wisdom passed down through generations and made relevant to the time we are now living in.

Great artists, writers, film-makers, actors, actresses, poets, songwriters, musicians and dancers have blessed the world with the sharing of their heart and soul through the media they felt most passionate about. So much inspired wisdom and personal stories are shared in this way. Most of us have gone to see a movie or read a book that has helped to change our perception in some way large or small. This may lead us into making different choices for ourselves and to change the very direction of our lives, like my experience of watching *The Butterfly Effect,* as mentioned in chapter 1!

Your creative expressions contain the power to raise the consciousness of humanity, to inspire others to make different, more meaningful choices for their lives; to make a difference in the world! Through your creative expression, other people are actually inspired by who you are choosing to *be*.

Watching other creative people inspires us to *be* more creative too. Being amongst people ready to open and express more of who they are through creativity helps us *all* to do the same. The old romantic image of the starving artist alone in their studio or office struggling to find inspiration to create their masterpiece is not true to how a creative life can be lived now.

In a world full of distractions, it's vital to carve out time alone to do your creative work and develop projects and ideas. It is equally important to spend time in groups, which are hotbeds of creative inspiration to fuel your life in *every* imaginable way! Everyone perceives the world in their own unique way *and* expresses their life experiences in a language unique to them within their 'bubbles'.[28] So when you join creative groups in the form of workshops, classes and courses, you can open yourself to being inspired by every single person in that group. You become stimulated by the creative journeys of others.

We can't possibly choose everything in life which is one reason we connect with each other. We find out from others what it's like to choose a certain path. We are given the opportunity to intuit whether it's something that we would also like to try. Often it's enough for us to experience it through someone else. We can use that to inspire our own journey, as well as find new creative combinations for our projects.

We are supporting each other and are the messengers, through the sharing of our words, our movies and books, our workshops, our songs and music, our businesses, our teleseminars and talks. We are supporting each other to make a move and take courageous steps towards following our dreams, to what we want to contribute to our world and how we want our lives to be. We live by example. Look to the life of the people who you are inspired by. What is it about their lives that inspire you?

---

[28] In chapter 12, Purpose, I explain what bubbles are in the way that I reference them here.

The Goddess of Pleasure touches our lives when we choose to do that which is most fulfilling to our souls.

The *Creative Self-Expression* Pleasure Project

In your Pleasure Project journal, write a list or create a video or a tactile creative project, of 5 creative people, books, movies, paintings, poems, songs or other creative expressions that have inspired and moved you throughout your life (If you want to make your list longer then do so, keep going until you can't think of anything else). Under each of the items you have listed, write what it was about the book, movie, etc. that inspired you so much. Was it the story? What thoughts or feelings did it provoke in you?

1. Creative people that have inspired me:

1.

2.

3.

4.

5.

What inspiration did these creative people give me?

2. Books that have inspired me:

1.

2.

3.

4.

5.

What inspiration did these books give me?

3. Movies that have inspired me:

    1.

    2.

    3.

    4.

    5.

What inspiration did these movies give me?

4. Poems, songs or music that have inspired me:

    1.

    2.

    3.

    4.

    5.

What inspiration did these poems, songs or music give me?

5. Other creative expressions that have inspired me:

What have you learnt about yourself through this Pleasure Project?

Look back at this list often, print it or paint it out and post it in a place where you will see it regularly, so that you remind yourself whom and what inspires you to stay on the creative path you want to be on. It will become a piece of the Language of the World that the universe will bring your attention to, in those moments you lose your way.

Chapter Summary

- Creativity has always been used as a healing tool to express the unexpressed
- Your creative expressions often reveal hidden emotions and thought patterns that you were not aware of
- The creative people you admire are your tribe
- Your creative expressions are powerful and have the potential to catalyse the lives of others and expand perception

CHAPTER NINE

The Language of Colour and Creating Yourself

Like rainbows, we have many colours to our personalities; we have co-lourful lives and colourful stories to tell. Each of us has a unique palette with which we can creatively play by accepting and enjoying the colourful physical attributes we have, which can include: brown skin, red hair, blue eyes, auburn hair, white skin, big orange freckles, green eyes, ebony skin, charcoal eyes, big brown afro hair, fine white hair, golden eyes, peach skin, lilac eyes, black glossy hair, olive skin, hazel eyes, dark scattered freckles, blonde curls, clear blue eyes, mocha skin, amber waves, fawn brown poker straight hair and so many other unique combinations.

Naturally, we are colourful and surrounded by a vast and terrific spectrum of colours in our world. Nature displays the richest and most diverse range of awe-inspiring colours through flowers, leaves and plants, trees, birds, insects, fish, oceans, sky and sunsets. The colour palette of the planet is magnificent. And man has tried to replicate these colours in many forms. But no man-made colour quite contains the depth, vibrancy and energy of nature's colours.

Everything on this planet contains some kind of colour, although black is said to be the absence of colour and defined as the visual impression experienced when no visible light reaches the eye, while white contains the entire spectrum of colours we see. The food we eat is colourful and we recognise when it's ripe to eat from its colour as well as its smell. Think of lemons, oranges, beetroot and carrots. Spinach, avocados, strawberries, blueberries, mangos or tomatoes; what an incredible rainbow of so many delicious colours. Our clothes, accessories and makeup, as well as the decor in our homes represent our colour tastes and often our moods. All advertising plays on the emotional response that research suggests we have to certain colours. Brands and countries become known for their colours. Think orange for Easy-Jet Airlines and the Netherlands. Some people look radiant when wearing certain colours, whereas others look dull or drained wearing that same colour.

When we connect more deeply with the rhythms of our body, we discover that everything in our world has an influence in our lives, which affects how we feel at any given moment. In this chapter, we explore the joy of colour, how to create yourself as art, show your language through your style and how the Language of the World speaks to us through colour.

CREATING YOURSELF

Creating yourself means taking a new stance on your beauty and body and cultivating deep nourishment, self-care and the great joy that you can feel 'creating yourself'. When you return to the art of creating your own unique style through the colours, fabrics, clothes, jewellery, shoes, accessories and makeup you choose to wear, you become the creative artist and the living art.

You can create and express who you are and what you feel through the way that you present yourself in life *and* have fun and take pleasure in doing so.

When you use natural, organic, mineral-based makeup, use it to enhance your features, to compliment the colour of your top or to match your shoes. Be the artist, be the creator of how you feel that day and how you would like to express that feeling through your body adornments and outer expression.

The indigenous peoples of the planet and our ancestors have always adorned and decorated their bodies with natural paints, jewels, stones, metals, feathers, beads, fabric and colour for different reasons; for spiritual ceremony, war and festive ceremonies as well as to accentuate and celebrate their bodies. Yet, many girls and women in our modern world use makeup to cover and hide their features and experience no pleasure in 'creating' themselves because as they are doing so, they feel little pleasure and an underlying anxiety about how they look. As they look in the mirror and apply makeup, they only see what they don't like about their appearance. They see what needs to be fixed. **When you look in the mirror each day, do you smile at what you see?** Or is your first thought always a negative one?

Creating yourself is art. How do you feel today? Feminine, flirty, fun, sexy, serious, tom-boyish, goddess-like, cosy, comfortable, energised, simple, eccentric? What colours and fabrics are you drawn to wear? How do you want to move? What accessories will you wear today that make you feel good?

We need to bring the joy, colour, creativity and pleasure back to our self-expression through style by playing with the unique version of beauty that we have. Our feminine element revels in this form of expression.

BEAUTY

What makes someone beautiful? We've all seen striking models and stunning women who on visual beauty alone fulfil a universal concept of what beauty looks like, although different cultures value different looks. Images of women with slim figures, toned stomachs, smooth flawless skin, beautiful breasts, pretty faces, long legs and lush hair are projected into our culture as the ideal version of beauty, but let's take a look at the deeper meaning of beauty.

What is *true* beauty? Beauty recognised leaves you breathless, in awe of its magnificence. You leave the presence of real beauty feeling uplifted and radiant; as if your universe has suddenly expanded. A vision of something beautiful can be shocking, it can melt your heart, leave you in disbelief and move you to tears. Real beauty touches deep emotional chords that surface beauty cannot reach. To the eyes and heart of someone who appreciates and understands true beauty, anything and anyone can touch them. Beauty is indeed in the eye of the beholder.

We can be blinded by physical beauty and begin to compare ourselves to the way others look. Comparison, as we all know, can be detrimental to appreciating and feeling pleasure in our own unique version of beauty. **It is both our external and internal beauty that create beauty's wholeness.** In the presence of true beauty, be that a person, a place, an object or a situation, there is no incentive to compare because beauty has touched the heart as well as the mind. We are not just 'in the mind' when we think about beauty; beauty has entered our being. It has accessed the division in our inner and outer worlds and changed us from within.

The language of our culture often drowns out the Language of the World, the language of our own internal wisdom, because we allow it to. We give the voices of society more precedence over our own voice, when in fact, it is our own voice and intuition that leads us to joy. It can feel very difficult and isolating to go against a cultural grain as individuals, collectively it is certainly easier. **Yet against the grain is where our evolution occurs, as we stretch into new ways of being and your voice is a part of this story.**

COLOUR

Colour subtly or strongly affects our emotional, energetic and physical wellbeing and this is how the Language of the World speaks to us through colour. Particularly to those of us who love to work and play with colour. Colour Therapists use colour as a catalyst to affect change in their clients but we can individually discover how to use colour for ourselves too. There are many factors which influence the way that we each perceive colour. People with regular vision see colour using three visual pigments of red, green and blue but people who are colour-blind only use two of these pigments. Some people are colour-deficient, which means the reception of one colour is misaligned. This results in reduced sensitivity to receive red, green or blue. Although very rare, there are some people who are completely colour-blind and only see one colour which is usually greyscale.

The physics of light also greatly affects the way that we each perceive colour because colour actually *is* light that travels in different wavelengths and frequencies. In a cold, dark climate, bright colours are not nearly as vibrant as they are in a place where the sun shines and the skies are blue. You may have noticed in hot climates, that most people dress in much brighter colours than they do in colder climates. The predominant colours worn in colder climates when we look into a crowd of people are generally very neutral; black, greys and darker, muted shades of other colours like burgundy, plum, burnt orange and brown. The sun does the task of amplifying the vibrancy of colour. We can see simply how colour changes when light flickers through a bedroom window enhancing the colour of the walls on the patches where it shines. Or when the sun shines on someone's hair or eyes, colours and multiple shades appear that we could not see when the clouds were covering the light.

The *quality* of light also changes the way we see colours. I don't know many people who enjoy the harshness of fluorescent lights in the supermarket that manage to highlight everyone's features and colouring in the worst possible way! Ambient lighting and soothing music would make shopping in supermarkets a much more enjoyable experience.

COLOUR AND EMOTION

Colour speaks to our emotions, the mechanics of colour is also a science, yet we don't need to fully understand the science behind colour, as fascinating as it is, to learn how colour can affect our lives. You can develop and learn to trust your own intuitive sense and association with colour and everything else through how you emotionally and physically respond to colours. Use the knowledge that is already in your DNA. The Encyclopaedia Britannica states, *"Artists and designers have been studying the effects of colours for centuries and have developed a multitude of theories on the uses of colour. The number and variety of these theories demonstrates that no universally accepted rules apply; the perception of colour depends on individual experience".*[29]

Similarly, if we want to explore the meaning of our dreams, we can learn how to practice conscious dreaming, rather than being guided by someone else's dream analysis in which we read their opinions and ideas of what our dreams mean to us. By tuning-in to *your* intuition, feelings and inner guidance, *you* can interpret and know what colours feel and mean to you, just as you can interpret your own dreams. If you choose to do research into the science of colours or dreaming, then you may find that it simply supports and expands what your intuition has already told you.

We each have our own associations, interpretations and emotional responses to colour, just as we do with certain pieces of music or imagery.

[29] The quote is used with permission from https://luminous-landscape.com/colour-theory/ via Encyclopaedia Britannica.

The Language of the World uses colour in the same way it uses symbols, words, images or any other 'tool', but colour also has the element of temperature.

There are many shades and hues in the colour spectrum that range in temperature. The primary or first-order colours are pure colours of red, yellow and blue. Every other colour in-between is a mix of any two or more of the primary colours. Cool colours include the palest shades of blues, violet, indigo and silver. Warm colours include pinks, oranges, yellow and red which is positively hot! White contains all colours in the spectrum, just as white noise can absorb all surrounding sound, and green is a balancing colour in the middle of the spectrum.

Each colour has a certain frequency or vibration which can affect the way that we feel. And the temperature of colours can have a 'warming' or 'cooling' effect on us.

Try the following simple visualisation and notice how your body and emotions respond to each colour.

Close your eyes and imagine yourself in a scarlet red room with natural light in which all four walls, roof and floor are red. Stand in the centre of the room and let the colour sink into you by breathing it in. How do you feel? Now, in the same way, imagine a black room and notice how your mood changes. Try this with a white room, a golden room or a pink room. Note the reaction of your body and the difference in what you feel after spending 5 minutes visualising being in each room.

The colours we choose to have in certain rooms at home influence how we feel being in that room. Most people are aware of the difference between warming and cooling colours and that it's probably more soothing to paint your bedroom a softer and more soothing shade of any colour, rather than fluorescent pink! There wouldn't be much sleep happening in that bedroom. Can you feel how powerfully colour affects us in this simple way?

In many of my workshops, we've worked with colour through painting to eventually form a spontaneous image or abstract art piece. Colour can have powerful healing effects as we go about intuitively choosing the colours we want to work with in that moment. Some participants may not have been fully conscious of it at the time, but the colours they worked with were subtly influencing them, healing[30] their energy bodies or affecting their mood.

The images or marks we create with colour are the languages of our mental, emotional, energetic and physical state in that moment. By looking at the marks we create with the colours we choose, we can begin to see a message that emerges in the moment, or sometimes a pattern, over a number of weeks, with regular practice of spontaneous expression through colour.

Perhaps one morning you feel drawn to wear a bright red cardigan as you get dressed. The colour seems very appealing to you that day and blatantly stands out in your wardrobe, it seems almost illuminated and very enticing. As you put the red cardigan on and look at yourself in the mirror, you have a sense of feeling strong and bold. You can feel the fiery energy of red energising you and helping you to stay grounded. You may even feel more energy at your root chakra and the lower half of your body. Wearing red helps you get into the energetic state you need to be in that day.

---

[30] This is a perfect example of how 'healing' can occur when we focus on what lights us up as discussed in chapter 2, page 42, The Forgotten Language of Pleasure.

What you actually experience from wearing red may be different than the example above as you will find out from completing the Pleasure Project at the end of this chapter.

Most of us also have a strong association with red as a signal to STOP. When the traffic lights turn red, we must stop and wait. Red is related to danger and emergency and in the animal kingdom, the male frigatebird inflates a huge red, balloon-like pouch at his throat as a way of attracting a mate, so red is also associated with attraction. The Language of the World uses your associations with and your emotional and physical response to colour as a tool to communicate with you.

There are many books that have been written on colour theory. If you'd like to delve deeper into this vast and complex subject try reading *Theory of Colours* by Goethe which was written in 1810. This book contains some of the earliest published descriptions of phenomena such as coloured shadows and refraction.

Begin to bring more awareness to the language of colour or lack thereof in your life, your home, your wardrobe and the way that you create yourself each day.

The *Colour and Creating Yourself* **Pleasure Project**

BEAUTY

Start collecting images and ideas that you want to use on your live canvas (that's you!).

When you wake up in the morning, think of yourself as a living, moving, blank canvas and tune-in to how you feel.

1. **What do you want to express about yourself today?**
   Do you feel edgy? Soft, inward, exhilarated, quiet?

2. **What does that look like for you when you express through creating yourself?** Is it a certain contrasting colour combination? A fresh hairstyle or colour? A familiar, trusty shoulder bag?

3. **What does true beauty mean to you? What does it look like?**

4. **How do you feel in the presence of true beauty?**

5. **What do you appreciate about your own unique version of beauty?**

You might begin with: "I love the way—*my hair feels soft and comforting*", or "*how graceful my movement is*", Or, "I love the—*colour contrast of my dark hair and pale skin*" or "*the small collection of freckles on my shoulders*".

Take the time to find something you truly appreciate about your look and expression whether you consider yourself to be a 'beauty' or not; there is beauty in every unique human expression. Begin with one aspect you notice about your appearance and continue appreciating more aspects you can admire.

COLOUR

1. Write a list of each colour in the spectrum as shown in the colour chart, in your Pleasure Project journal. Try to just take note of the colours without reading my own associations with them first so that you are clearer when tuning-in to how you feel about them yourself.

2. Take a few minutes to imagine and feel each colour, or find a piece of clothing or an object that contains the colour. Tune-in to how you feel in relation to each colour and notice how your body and emotions may respond.

3. Write down all the words, feelings and memories that appear to you for each colour and where you have seen and felt this colour. Keep the list when you are done, as a chart to refer to, to remind you of the colours that make you feel good or uplift you, make you feel sexy or empowered, feminine, open, closed, warm, happy, melancholic, natural, alive or energised.

You can use this chart when buying new clothes and home furnishing, jewellery or art to create the feeling you want to enhance. But be warned, I once thought that bright yellow would be a great colour to paint my bedroom when I was a student in art school. After a week of sleeping in the room, I began to get headaches because the colour was so bright it over stimulated my mind and I couldn't sleep properly! I felt much more at peace in the lilac bathroom.

COLOUR CHART

Red	Energetic, alive, vibrant, juicy, hot, explosive, sexy, base, root, dangerous, warning, stop, emergency, bold.
Shades of Red	Burgundy, maroon, cherry, pink.
Pink	Nurturing, soft, compassion, love, openness, gentle, heart, motherly, baby.
Shades of Pink	Magenta, fuchsia, Barbie pink, hot pink, rose pink, pale pink.
Orange	Healing, autumn, sacral, rich, grounding, citrus, sunset, vitamin C.
Shades of Orange	Peach, tangerine, coral.
Yellow	Mind, intellectual, confidence, sunshine, daffodils, buttercups, solar plexus, power.
Shades of Yellow	Lemon, pale yellow (lack of confidence, summery, soft, girl), cream, mustard.
Gold	High consciousness, wealth, royalty, refined intellect, treasure, precious metal.
Green	Heart, emotions, nature, expansive, home, calming, fertile, lush.
Shades of Green	Mint green, forest green, lime green, emerald green, olive green, turquoise.
Blue	Creativity, expression, communication, throat, peace, cool, passive, water, sky, baby boys, expansive.
Shades of Blue	Royal blue (elegant, classic, queen), sky blue (freedom, expansive, light, aeroplanes, flying, travel), navy blue, turquoise.
Purple	Spiritual, deep, connected, mysterious, mystic.
Shades of Purple	Indigo (higher consciousness, nobility, warmth), lilac (soft, calming, soothing, tranquil, lavender, heather), violet.
Brown	Grounding, earth, root, real, soil, forests, mud.
Shades of Brown	Beige, copper, rust (desert, New Mexico, metal), chocolate (rich, velvety, dark, luxurious, sweet, sensual, smooth).
White	Pure, infinite, consciousness, light, expansive.
Black	Dark, solid, bold, mysterious, sexy, dense, slimming, endless, hole, blind.
Shades of Black	Grey (depressing, melancholy, in-between, not clear, slate, stone, cold, cloudy, Aberdeen, Scotland), silver (light, ethereal, elegant, cool, sterile, metallic, precious, alien).

■ Chapter Summary

- You can 'create yourself' as a living, breathing, walking piece of art
- Express your feelings through your style
- Allow in the Goddess of Pleasure as you enjoy creating yourself
- Appreciate your unique, natural colour palette; this is your canvas
- Allow true beauty to move your emotions
- Stop comparing yourself with other people, learn to appreciate your unique version of beauty
- Colour affects how we feel: be aware of the colours in your home and wardrobe and notice how they make you feel
- Trust your own intuitive, physical, mental and emotional response to colour

CHAPTER TEN

The Language of Music and Sound

The pleasure music and sound bring to our lives can be profound. Music is powerful, gentle, complex, beautiful, invigorating, calming and soothing. It can push buttons, bring up memories from the past, release, heal, open and inspire. Music can wash away worry like a musical waterfall and envelop you in warmth and comfort like a soft blanket. Certain sounds can soothe and uplift the soul. Music is imbued with emotion by the singer, the songwriter, each instrument and its personality as well as the story in the lyrics. Music is rich with meaning and has the power to influence and even change the direction of our lives.

COMMUNICATING WITH MUSIC

Music and sound are astounding tools of communication. The shamans of Hawaii and Polynesia used drumming as a form of communication as well as to maintain rhythm and energise themselves and others. Using the medium of music as a language is very powerful because it speaks directly to our emotions and so the impact of music can be very deep. Our bodies can feel the vibration of music and respond to it intuitively, if we allow it. Music is a strong language and an excellent, clear and powerfully transformative tool when understood as a Language of the World.

From the sounds of nature, the elements, oceans, animals and birds to the first sound of our mother's heartbeat while in the womb to the vast and varied music composed by songwriters and the everyday sounds of life; cars, hoovers, the hum of the city; there are billions of sounds in the world.

Often, the sounds you hear can alert your attention and bring your awareness back to the present moment. The sound of a dog barking loudly and spontaneously can snap you from your daydreams. Consider this a gift. Anytime you are taken back to the present moment with a sudden or subtle sound, be it wind chimes tinkling, a car horn honking, someone sneezing, a waiter dropping a tray of cups, an alarm going off, your neighbour playing the violin—you get the picture—you are brought back to the now moment, the present. The present moment is where you need to be to fully experience your own life. So next time you become aware of these sounds, consider them a wake-up blessing, even if they did give you a jolt.

THERE'S NO SUCH THING AS SILENCE

In my e-zines, I like to share inspiring, informative and joyful tips and tools with my audience that will make a difference in the way they navigate through their day. In one blog post, I mentioned an article from an edition of *The Guardian Weekend* magazine, based on an interview with George Michelson Foy. It's called, *I've Been to the Quietest Place on Earth*.[31] Foy's search for peace and quiet leads him to the anechoic chamber at Orfield Laboratories, in Minnesota, USA. This chamber or room is designed to completely absorb the reflection of sound or electromagnetic waves and is the Guinness World Record's quietest place on earth; 99.9 percent sound absorbent. Foy's research shows that most people cannot stand to

---

[31] Read the full article online at http://www.theguardian.com/lifeandstyle/2012/may/18/experience-quietest-place-on-earth.

be in the room for more than a few minutes. This is because spending time in the chamber induces a sense of fear, since people are deprived of the usual reassuring ambient sounds of life. He also discovers, from 45 minutes spent in the room, that there is no such thing as silence! Due to the lack of any other sound, he becomes acutely aware of his own bodily sounds. His breath, the blood rushing through his veins and the skin moving over his scalp. He also hears a strange metallic scraping sound and thinks he has begun hallucinating. Foy concludes that you'd have to be dead to experience absolute silence. And then that depends on what you think happens when you die!

We are *never* truly in silence in terms of sound. And if it were possible to experience complete and utter silence, having lived in a world filled with sound, we would at first, after a much shorter time than you'd imagine, become seriously disturbed. **The sounds of the world we hear around us every day and night reassure us of life on Earth.** If there were no birds singing, no wind in the trees, no hum of electrical appliances or the crunch of soil beneath our feet, then we might feel as if there were no life on the planet. So if we look, or rather listen to sound, we can experience the power of its healing effects and feel its comforting warmth that soothes and protects us. Whether that is the general sounds of activity on Earth, nature or our own singing, toning or chanting; the sounds of life remind us that we are ALIVE and are part of the Language of the World.

SONG

One of my favourite ways of listening and communicating with the Language of the World is through songs and song lyrics. From a very early age, I dreamt of being a songwriter. This vehicle of expression is very powerful and brings me close to my own core essence. It's a language that I love and so it's clear to me why I receive so much inspiration, messages and guidance through song, lyrics and poetry. The tools of poetry and song also integrate the heart and the intellect, which loves to be stimulated as well. If we follow what we love and what lights us up, we can hear the clearest guidance in the most joyful ways.

There have been many times when I've heard a song and become particularly aware of the lyrics and the message that they gave me. I might find myself singing the words and melody of a song that I was not even aware I was singing. Or a song will just pop into my mind without me having thought it before. I become alert and listen more intently to the words, which often reflect my thoughts. I usually find they are very meaningful to me at that present moment and therein lies the message.

Perhaps you have a gift for writing your own songs and a message comes to you as you write. If you share your music and songs with others, *your* words could be the Language of the World conversing with someone else. *Your* song could be the catalyst for change in someone's life.

Below, I share a special moment in which I clearly heard the Language of the World communicating through song:

One day in early 2012, while in Scotland, I felt an inner sadness connected to feeling alone. In moments when I feel unclear or melancholy, I often find a place in nature to sit in solitude. I found a beautiful spot overlooking a river where I sat on a rock and felt my sadness. I sat in stillness by the river for some time and then a melody popped into my head. I recognised the melody, but couldn't remember the song lyrics. I sang it over and over and had a feeling it was a song written by the Scottish band, 'Snow Patrol'. After a while, I heard the words 'light up', which I thought were some of the lyrics from the chorus. I returned home later that afternoon and Googled 'Snow Patrol' with the words 'light up'. Their song, titled Run appeared. I looked up the lyrics and as I read them, tears poured down my face. The Language of the World spoke to me through the words of the song. One line of lyrics particularly stood out. It said:

'Light up, light up, as if you have a choice, even if you cannot hear my voice, I'll be right beside you dear'.[32]

I felt an incredibly loving, energetic presence by my side when I read those words and felt so supported and embraced in that moment.

These experiences can often feel difficult to explain to other people, especially when they are so deeply meaningful and potent to us. We can choose to keep them close, like a sacred secret, as described in chapter 2, The Forgotten Language of Pleasure, or share with close friends whom we know will resonate. Yet I often find that when shared in a wider context, reading of others' similar experiences can be comforting and supportive of our individual sense of 'reality'. These moments are also opportunities for us to trust the knowingness within ourselves, to own our truth and live it by understanding that whatever we experience as our reality *is* as true for us as the 'reality' that we can tangibly touch, see and hear.

MUSIC AS AN ORACLE

Just as we pick angel, tarot or oracle cards to offer clarity, guidance and

---

[32] Snow Patrol, 'Run', *Final Straw*, Rec. February 2003, Fiction/Polydor, January 2004.

communication from our inner source in co-creation with the universe; music can work in the same way. If you find your attention dwelling on a person or situation in your life that you want clarity on, you can use music as an oracle. There are a number of ways to use music and song as an oracle. The first way is as described in my story above. When you find yourself spontaneously singing a song or when lyrics significantly stand out through the speakers, when you're shopping in the supermarket or out and about, truly listen. Listen carefully to the words, there may be an important message from your inner source and the universe within them.

With oracle cards, you shuffle them and either spread them out to pick one or two, or you cut the deck and pick the card or cards on top. Using music as an oracle really works best when you have a 'shuffle' option, as we have on iPods and iTunes. This way of using music as an oracle is good if you have a specific question, person or situation you'd like clarity on. Often, I just have a feeling I should listen to some music to lighten my day and it reflects exactly what I've been thinking about. Follow the Pleasure Project at the end of this chapter to use the music oracle.

VOICE

The source of music and sound also emerges from each and every human being and animal. The human voice has been described as one of the most powerful and beautiful, natural musical instruments there is. Our voices are capable of so much more than we use them for, individually and collectively they hold great power. Sound and voice expert, Jill Purce, says, ***"As we become more developed, we become more silent, there is great***

need for us to restore our voices".[33]

In my video interview with Jill Purce, she explains why working with the voice, specifically in overtone chanting, can be transformational. *"When we chant overtones, we are turning our bodies into a musical instrument of a very powerful, resonant kind; more so than when we normally sing. In this kind of chanting, we are producing the essence of resonance with the most essential and powerful aspect of sound itself, the pure harmonics.*

By doing this, we're working with the energy body and transforming that by eliminating confusion and blockages in the mind; things that impinge on the clarity of our awareness. Most sickness starts with a disturbance in the energy body, this then moves into the emotional and then physical body. The more we work with the energy body, the more profound the changes that can happen. If we leave it until something physical manifests, it's too late to change anything because it's the end of the chain. We need to give ourselves a sonorous massage before the effects reach the physical body".*

Jill states that western music is out of tune, whereas overtone chanting, originating from central Asia and yet non cultural, is in-tune. She believes that in listening to western music we begin to resonate out of tune with ourselves, with our own internal geometry, with nature, and the world. And instead of being sound in mind, voice and body, we are actually being distorted. Jill shares that working with vocal overtones is a way for us to re-tune, so we can be sound in mind and body. She also calls working with the voice 'Vocal Yoga'* because we are working with the breath and this brings us into deep states of meditation in which we can move into a very magical and still place within ourselves.

Animals also love the sound of overtone chanting and can hear a wider

---

*[33] Quote taken from a personal interview with Jill Purce; Part One and Part Two can be viewed on my blog here: http://www.janecormack.com/video-audio/ and on YouTube here: https://www.youtube.com/watch?v=W7W1g_il4aI and Part Two here: http://youtu.be/S9ZnEZtcUkE.

range of notes than humans can. We can connect on a very deep level with animals through sound.

When we listen to live music, as opposed to recorded music, this adds many more elements to our musical experience and fills a space in a very different way. The personality of the singers and musicians in the room become involved, how they handle the instruments they play, as well as what mood they are in that day all influence the sounds they put together in the moment. Sometimes, if all the stars align in the sky, magic happens. It's spontaneous and thrilling to witness a live, magical musical moment.

OPENING THE BODY THROUGH SOUND

It's also possible to visually 'see' music. And I don't mean musical notes on paper. Sound and music cause vibration. When sand is exposed to sound, it creates different patterns. The higher the vibration of sound, the more complex the pattern is that appears in the sand. Sound can also be seen in water because sound has a structure. Given that sound has a vibrational effect on matter, it also affects the human body in different ways in response to the type of sound we are exposed to. This is one way that sound can help to recalibrate or heal the body.

We can make various manner of sounds emerge from different parts of our bodies and give 'voice' to these parts to help open and release energy, in the form of emotion that is 'stuck' there. In western culture, we have primarily learned to create sound from the waist up because that's where the majority of our focus is and why as a result, so much tension is held in the shoulders, neck and head. This creates a thinner, weaker sound because we are not using the power and force of our whole body and energy. When we connect with our solar plexus, which is the centre of our power, and try to create sound from where our diaphragm is, the sound becomes deeper, more resonant and full. We can feel our own power emerging through the sound moving through our bodies and begin to feel a more balanced flow of energy as our bodies begin to open. For women, we can sound the 'voice' of our deepest feminine essence connected to and held within our wombs. We can release old wounds connected to our sexuality and heal the physical and emotional body through opening to sound. Practicing toning can help us find out where we are creating the sound from. Toning in a group is a great way to play around with different sounds that we may not realise we can make as well as weave into the sounds of other voices.

Working with the voice and sound can have immediate and dramatic results because our whole being is re-activated and revved up. We feel more alive, have more vitality, posture can improve, communication is clearer and we can become generally more open, grounded, radiant and confident in expressing ourselves.

Music, song, voice and sound contain powerful energy and messages for humanity. Think of the famous song, *Man in the Mirror,* by Michael Jackson. He got it so right when he said in his song, *"I'm starting with the man in the mirror, I'm asking him to change his ways",* [34] and *"If you want to make the world a better place, take a look at yourself and make the change".* This song, along with many other Michael Jackson songs, contains potent messages for humanity. The change begins with us and as Gandhi famously said, *"Be the change that you wish to see in the world".* [35]

---

[34] Jackson, Michael, 'Man in the Mirror', *'Bad'*. Rec. February – May 1987. Epic 1988.

[35] Mahatma Gandhi.

The *Music and Sound* Pleasure Project

THE MUSIC ORACLE

1. Take out your Pleasure Project journal and a pen. Go to the 'songs' option on your iPod or click the shuffle option on iTunes or similar. This gives you the option to shuffle every single song from all the albums you have.

2. Think of a specific question, person or situation you'd like clarity on.

3. Press shuffle and wait for the first song to start. Listen carefully to the lyrics of the song as well as the melody. It's usually through the lyrics that the message is given but you may also feel the effects on your energy and physical body through the melody. It may be just one line of the entire song that elicits an emotional response from you, makes you smile, laugh or cry, or it could be the first or last verse. It may even be the second song that comes through the shuffle that speaks to you more directly than the first. So leave the music playing for the first few songs to really get the message.

   I've often found that the first few songs are on a related subject but give me different perspectives on it. So this way of asking for guidance can be more in-depth than using any kind of oracle card. It's also a lot of fun.

4. Look lyrics up online, write them in your journal and look at which parts of the lyrics felt significant to you or that you found yourself singing again and again. The message in the song will speak to your emotions. It's often simply reassuring and comforting to hear in the moment or like any form of the Language of the World, the music oracle may guide you to make a bigger decision to move forward with your life.

Chapter Summary

- Music is a powerful tool for communication
- There's no such thing as silence, enjoy the ambient sounds of life on Earth
- Notice when the Language of the World speaks to you through song
- Play the music oracle
- Our collective voices have great power to affect change
- The world needs the power of YOUR voice to be heard
- Sound causes vibration that can affect your body
- Music contains potent messages for humanity

CHAPTER ELEVEN

The Language of Word and Symbols

A book illuminated on a shelf; you pull it out, open it randomly and read a poem—it's as if that poem were written just for you, in that specific moment. Whatever you are going through, the words you have read have offered you solace. They have comforted you, enveloped you in a tangible energy that has somehow penetrated your heart and filled you with that God-like love. Your puffed out chest is now trembling with the knowing that you are connected to and are part of a universe that knows you, that feels you, that speaks with you. A universe that listens. A universe you hold within. In that moment, you know you are not alone, that you never have been and although you'll forget again and again in your moments of sorrow, deep pain, hardship and heartbreak; the knowing is eternally present.

WORD

Words may be your wanderlust; a prolific pleasure map that guides you deeper into the truth and source of who you are. Words are your way to adventure, to travel off-piste, to swim into the dark oceans of other people's lives. **Words are the curves that carve deep, they weave the poetry of who you are into the tapestry of existence.** Words may be your gold and diamonds, slicing through the rusted tin that is the daily waffle, the skimming-the-surface word exchange that counts as connection. In moments, we can capture those shining flecks of gold amongst the pan of grit and sometimes we find a nugget. That nugget is more than a word; it's a purely inspired idea that becomes an expression of you and an expression of something bigger than you, beyond you. Words can be plumped with pleasure, filled out and focused. They can also be dry drivel droning on, splitting our hearts and heads like a knife edge.

PURE GOLD—THE CREATORS FRUSTRATION

That moment, you're in the zone, connected to source and pluck out a piece of pure gold. It's so precious, divine, illuminated and clear and you desperately want to find a way to capture it and—

PURE GOLD

Words in my head,
pure gold
falling to silver,
bronze,
turning to copper,
rusting,
forming,
escaping
like wood chip.[36]
—Jane Alexandra Cormack

[36] Cormack, Jane, 'Poems of Earth, Heart & Spirit', unpublished dissertation, 2009.

That gold gets filtered through your being, your mind and your body and oftentimes emerges in a very different way than you may have imagined. Sometimes, the results feel like they are far removed from their origins, much to the frustration of many artists. And yet, it is the energy behind the words and the essence of you that remains, regardless of whether you dismiss your art as terrible or not. Through all of our expressions, we are capturing a feeling and energy, and this is what other people, your tribe, can sense and see. This essence filters through the editing process and ideas of perfectionism and restructuring, shuffling around, a piece here and piece there, stick it all together like a jigsaw puzzle and there we go; the final product, the end result. After all that poking and prodding, the underlying message still gets through because it was there from the start.

Like capturing a shoal of fish in a net, we gather words to hold the energy of what it is we really mean to communicate. The book you now hold in your hands, feeling and reading, are the words I collected in my net to form a structure around the essence of my message. Words are tools for us to play with, like everything else that is the Language of the World.

The Language of the World speaks to us so prolifically through the written word and is one of the clearest and most direct ways for us to receive this universal communication. They can be words found in books and book titles, magazines, flyers, posters, online and on car number/word plates; words on labels, shop windows, a text, on TV, in greetings cards, a business card, a CD cover, poetry—anything that has words or symbols on it. Letters and words appear in all manner of formats. Words can be prolific, flowing, simple, direct, spoken, written, heard and painted.

SCIENCE OF THE WORD

The process of how our brains connect and respond to certain words and story is fascinating. Neuroscience research[37] has discovered that reading stories, such as fictional novels can stimulate different parts of the brain and can actually influence how we behave. The language-processing areas of our brains are activated, along with many other parts, including those areas devoted to dealing with smells. This explains why the experience of reading fiction can feel so alive. Parts of our brain believe the emotional exchange between characters in a fictional novel is real.

When we read words such as 'cinnamon' or 'lavender' our sense of smell is stimulated through our olfactory cortex in the brain. And our sensory cortex is responsible for receiving texture through touch but also responds to reading textural words such as, 'her velvety voice' or 'his leathery hands'. Certain words will stimulate other parts of our brain creating emotional and/or physical responses through our bodily senses.

In chapter 9, on colour, you may very well have noticed that you 'saw' the colour in your mind's eye when you read the word 'yellow'. When we read the word 'yellow', it's very common to also 'see' the colour *and* to feel an emotional response to it. If we add the word 'lemon' to it and read it as 'yellow lemon' (try saying it really fast, out loud, several times!) most people will visualise the fruit of a yellow lemon and many people may also experience the sensory stimulation of taste. Experiencing sensory connections like this is also known as synaesthesia.

Such are the power of words, eliciting emotional and even physical responses. In this respect, the Language of the World works in multiple ways and in many different layers through the word. Through reading books, we

---

[37] Paul, Annie Murphy, 'Your Brain on Fiction' *The New York Times Sunday Review* online: http://www.nytimes.com/2012/03/18/opinion/sunday/the-neuroscience-of-your-brain-on-fiction.html?_r=0.

can actually enter into other people's thoughts, feelings and experiences.

When you read a book, you feel the energetic and sensory meaning of the words first, before your intellect connects with the actual word structure. The language of consciousness arrives *before* the words do.

THE MAGIC OF POETRY

Poetry becomes magical if we think about it related to neuroscience and the way certain words stimulate our senses. Many poets are so sparing in their use of words that a poem can become a concentrated, visually, emotionally stimulating rocket!

Cognitive neurologists from the medical school at the University of Exeter are working with new brain imaging technology and are beginning to prove that poetry is like music to the mind. Their research carried out a study on volunteers from their Psychology and English departments, in a specific comparison between poetry and prose. Evidence showed that poetry activated certain areas of the brain linked to introspection and memory. More emotionally charged writing aroused several areas of the brain, predominantly on the right side, which also respond to music.[38]

Poetry is also a fantastic tool to deeply connect with nature and our own source. Through writing or reading poetry, we can focus, in minute detail, on a particular subject or object. In doing so, we are really meditating on the subject or object of our focus. We are giving it attention.

There are many poets or 'nature poets' who focus on nature to inspire their writing. Mary Oliver is one of my favourites. Focusing attention on a plant, flower or rock allows us to feel it. In *feeling* it, we are in fact commu-

---

[38] Zeman, Adam; Milton, F.; Smith, A.; Rylance, R, 'By Heart An fMRI Study of Brain Activation by Poetry and Prose'. *Journal of Consciousness Studies*, Imprint Academic, Volume 20, Numbers 9-10, 2013, pp. 132-158(27).

nicating with the consciousness of the plant and speaking the Language of the World.[39]

Poetry can also reveal the truth of a person in a direct or indirect way. Many poets and songwriters bare their soul in their work, because the act of writing poetry becomes like a portal into the depths of their heart. This shows us the essence of who they are and this is the important part of what we share with each other. What the poet or songwriter may really want to communicate is revealed in its purest form through their work. I love poetry and song that carries this essence of truth. It is the written experience of the poet or songwriter's story in connection with something divine.

I have personally been influenced by the Persian poet, Hafiz, who was a Sufi[40] poet. The poems of Hafiz, his fellow Persian poet, Rumi (1207-1273) and Indian poet Kabir (1440-1518) known as 'Poet Seers' or 'Mystic Poets' are *"A progression through intricacies of love and longing in the ultimate quest for truth".*[41] It is the transcendence of language and time that draws people to the mystic poets, because we are invited through their poetry, to join them on their personal journey to truth. Many of us are on this journey to our personal truth, which we can discover through our own creativity. Language, therefore, becomes a tool of initiation, a catalyst, if you will, which we can transcend to return to and discover the essence and the divine within it.

---

[39] Watch my video and read the blog post 'How to Meditate with Creative Expression' here: http://www.janecormack.com/rhythmic-inspiration-news/how-to-meditate-with-creative-expression/ (In it I talk about using a flower and poetry to meditate).

[40] A Sufi is a mystic in search of God.

[41] Cormack, Jane, *'Poems of Earth, Heart & Spirit'*, p124, unpublished dissertation, 2009.

SYMBOLS

Symbolism is an entire language in itself. In ancient times, symbols were often used as a language to communicate information secretly that would have caused great controversy, alienation or even death had it been communicated directly.

Symbols are rich in meaning, mythology and theology. There are millions of ancient and traditional symbols, such as the famous universal symbol of the spiral. The symbol of the spiral is found in the natural world in a myriad of ways including; spiral galaxies, nautilus shells and whirlpools of water as well as in the double helix structure of the human DNA molecule. The spiral is also thought to be the way that energy rises up the spine through the energy centres of the body. This is called 'Kundalini', which is the *Sanskrit* word for spiral or 'coiled energy'. In yogic and spiritual traditions, the spiral symbolises spiritual development to higher consciousness and the movement of energy. It is the symbol of the eternal, creative and organisational principle at work in the universe.

The entire Language of the World can be considered symbolic. Symbols are signs and the Language of the World speaks to us through these signs every day. We can and are in communication all the time, but we don't need to *think* about it all the time. If we did, then we'd probably go a bit crazy, over-analysing every single thing that emerges in our day *and* we'd spend way too much time caught up in our minds. The intellect is not the place from which we will initially 'get' or understand this language.

Noticing a sign may start with some aspect of the sign standing out to you. It can begin with a feeling, while seeing, hearing or touching this sign can have an initial impact on you as well, even if it's something you've seen/heard/touched thousands of times before. This specific time, something about the sign stops you in your tracks. You get a feeling and a knowing within that there's something new to pay attention to. Every form of communication in the Language of the World contains symbolism whether it's a colour, number, word, a part of nature, a song, an animal or a person. The signs that are presented to you are symbolic, they can be interpreted by you *and* can guide you to just what you need at that very moment. These symbols are like signposts or 'breadcrumbs' that highlight and lead you on a specific path, perhaps to a wonderful opportunity or to meet a certain person.

The following is a simple example from my own experience, of what listening to everyday signs and symbols can lead to:

A few years ago, while I was visiting Kauai, Hawaii, my attention was consistently brought to trees and branches in the shape of the letter Y. I must have seen a million Y-shaped twigs, trees and branches in my life and never paid any attention to them. But, this time, they really stood out to me and I felt that they meant something. My attention continued to be insistently drawn to the letter Y in the form of branches and trees for a number of days. I could have quite easily dismissed these symbols, yet something about the Y-shaped trees seemed illuminated and vibrant to me, as if they were jumping out from a plain backdrop. My mind began to try to interpret what this meant. Did it stand for Yes? Say Yes to life? Something Yellow!? Oh, I don't know! And so I just let it go.

Eventually, the answer came when I met a man during a powerful spiritual ceremony on a beach, whose first name began with the letter Y. I even saw him write his name in the sand with a big letter Y to show someone how to spell his name, which I would have thought began with an 'E'. When I saw the giant Y, I thought, 'hmmm'. The Language of the World was clearly communicating to me to pay attention to Mr Y when he came along! After the ceremony, we connected *and soon began a relationship that was transformative for both of us in many ways. It was a very intense, beautiful and challenging romance on the island of Kauai; the universe didn't want me to miss the opportunity to connect with Mr. Y.*

Try to stay open to exploring the nature of symbols that are illuminated in your daily life and make notes in your Pleasure Project journal. Paying attention to this language can lead us into the most extraordinary experiences and connections.

The log cabin I sit in now whilst writing this paragraph has a row of Y-shaped twigs on the mantelpiece because the surname of my friends who rent the cabin begins with a Y!

The *Word and Symbol* Pleasure Project

THE WORD ORACLE

1. Go to your bookshelf or if you don't have one, a library or bookstore.

2. Think of a situation or question that you need support with or would like clarity on and ask yourself *and* the universe this question.

3. Look at the bookshelves and notice which book or books 'stand out'. It might look illuminated or have a strong presence on the shelf.

4. Pick out that book and intuitively open it in the way that feels right to you. Randomly, look at the page or maybe a paragraph and see what lines 'pull you in'. You might be drawn to a paragraph or sentence or even a word and this is your message. It may not be what you imagined or expected, but its message is specifically shown to you in that moment.

5. Notice how receiving this message changes your perception, or gives you an idea or helps you to change your emotional state.

1. **How has the Language of the World been speaking to you through words and symbols?**

2. **What words or symbols have you noticed in your environment that stood out in the last two months and what message did they give you?**

DELICIOUS WORDS

In your Pleasure Project journal or right here in this book, write your immediate emotional response to these two lists of words below. Notice in your body, what senses are ignited as you read each word. Witness how the Language of the World stimulates your senses through words.

Chocolate	Velvet
Lavender	Leather
Cinnamon	Bark
Strawberry	Steel
Rose	Concrete
Mint	Wood
Coconut	Glass

Chapter Summary

- The universe communicates clearly and powerfully through words
- It's the energy behind the words in a book or poem that touches us
- Symbols are rich with meaning but listen to your own intuitive 'hit' when you notice symbols
- If you feel guided to find out more, do some research, hidden languages are often revealed

Part Four

CHAPTER TWELVE

The Language of Purpose

Your unique place in the world is like a map that spans through time and space. The 'map' of you is brought into existence when you are born on this planet. And your map's design has been created through the timelines of your ancestral line, the place and country you were born into, your parent's nationalities, your languages and accent, your emotional make-up, how you see the world and how you relate to people in it. There is NO ONE on earth like you. And there never will be—ever.

YOUR ESSENCE IS YOUR MAP—THE BIG PICTURE

The imprint of your essence creates an impact in the world, regardless of whether you think of yourself as quiet and small or loud and big. It is your unique map and is expressed through every fiber of your being. Your vocal timbre, the way you speak, the lilts and singsong of your voice, the speed at which you express yourself, your hair, your body, the way that you move when you walk or dance, the sound of your laugh and how your eyes almost close when you smile. Your unique imprint is embedded in your presence, your radiance, it's in your style and how you create yourself on the outside, it's your smell, the texture of your skin, how you write loopy or can memorise the names of everyone in your class. It's the colours you can and cannot see, it's the recipes you learned from your mother that you add your own flavour to. Your map includes what lights you up and makes you laugh as well as what makes you want to tear your hair out and scream in frustration. It's your shyness and vulnerability in social situations, the awkward way you try to say what you think, your tendency for swearing when you're nervous, your teapot collection, your joy of spontaneously spouting poetry on street corners or the breath that moves through your saxophone creating sound that only you could make. It's the way you love your child, how you like the clothes in your wardrobe to be in colour order or your obsession with all things French. It's what moves and thrills you. It's who you are. All of you. And your number one purpose on the planet is to be just that. Your contribution in the world comes through you being exactly who you are. I mean, right now, who you are.

Through being just who you are and all that that is, you are drawn by your desires to what is in your unique 'bubble' of a world. You attract reflections and mirrors of your essence and being, which you perceive in the people, experiences, opportunities, abundance and relationships that arrive in your reality. If, what you want is clear and simple, not vague and unsure, you tend to get clear and simple. If your desires are many and often changing, life may mirror that.

Look back a few years and remember what you felt then, what you longed for and feared. Have you since experienced some of those desires or wants fulfilled? Or have your fears made you feel like you hit a brick wall? By focusing on our fears, they can also begin to grow bigger in our imagination and we have the ability to call them into our reality just as we do our greatest visions and dreams. It is possible to feel your fear and acknowledge that it's there, while focusing on your deepest wants.

You may be able to biologically clone yourself (please don't), yet that clone of you would be like a diluted version of you. You are an intricate map of the sum of your life experiences, your beliefs, habits and feelings, your parents, your DNA, your country and culture and your ancestral lineage that stems back to our collective origins in Africa. There has been nobody who has walked the Earth like you and your purpose is to bring that to the planet. **Your purpose is to bring the sum of you forward into the human experience.** You don't have to force and deliberately share you. You do it naturally by *being* you. In the way that you are you.

EXPRESSING YOUR PURPOSE—THE PRACTICAL PART

This is where your unique essence meets practical, 'in the world' inspired action and movement. You can choose to share your essence and love through joy, the 'purpose' of you, which is all that you are. This is brought forward through the outward expression of you. And this could happen in so many ways. The 'purpose' of you can come through your words, a book perhaps, like this one, the food you prepare, how you read and carefully (or not), mark your students essays, the film script you write, the paintings you paint, how you lead groups, what you create through your challenges, your blog posts and photographs or the way you climb the ships masts as you sail out to sea. Your 'purpose' of you comes through what you do with joy, whatever you choose that to be.

Often our greatest creative achievements are born of our challenges and difficulties in doing them, along with our joy. When you choose the path of joy and pleasure in your work, even when the difficult times arise, and they will, the undercurrent of joy remains because you know you are on 'track' to the most expansive and fulfilling path for you.

Your purpose is to drink life in until you're overflowing so that you can water life with your being. Like the cycle of rain pouring on Earth, soaked up by the soil and then evaporated back up to the clouds, you drink in and water all of life. This is your purpose. And you can choose to do this in any form.

Your singing voice may be the gift that waters life, uplifting and deeply moving others emotionally. Your words and poetry may connect you to the depths of your heart and are a catalyst to propel people to follow their dreams. Your architectural designs bring you into connection with the language of who you are and infuse a practical beauty on the planet. The way you dance and move energy through your body is breathtaking to watch and cracks open closed hearts. The intricacy of your mind connects new, unseen patterns through numbers or symbols that contribute to human or technological evolution. **If it calls to you then bring it, do it, be it.**

BUBBLES

Bubbles describe the illusion that we all live in separate universes, as well as the languages we use within them. In chapter 5, Love & Relationships, I talked about how we can become trapped in our own bubbles and the importance of moving through different bubbles to stay balanced. Your job is a bubble and your family and friends are a bubble. A bubble contains your environments, all the people in them, the classes you go to, the kind of books you read and generally everything else that makes up your individual world. And you may be very aware or happily unaware of what goes on outside of it. Within your bubble is your unique map, the imprint of your essence. I use the term 'bubbles' because bubbles represent how we contain ourselves in protective yet permeable fields of energy that have the ability to cluster together, move lightly and freely around and ... burst.

Most of us have had the experience where we feel drawn to learn something new, like going to a class to learn a new skill or craft. When we begin on that path, entirely new worlds or bubbles we never knew existed open up to us. The deeper we delve into our chosen subject, the more we uncover and discover something new for ourselves that has been part of the world for much longer. Most of us move in, out and between different bubbles throughout our lives when we meet new people or are introduced to new situations. And some people never leave their bubble throughout their lives, either because they love it so much, or because they feel scared to leave the security, comfort and familiarity of what they know.

There are specific 'languages' that are contained within these bubbles in different industries and communities. In any new job or experience, there is a new language which you must learn if you want to do the job well and be understood. There is the language of science that those of us who don't work in the world of science may not understand. As we go deeper into the world and language of science, we will discover or rather uncover further specialised languages within the areas of chemistry, biology and neurology or quantum physics. And the deeper we go into each of these sectors, the more specialised and complex the language becomes.

The same can be said of Information Technology. There are various IT languages that many of us only know the basics of. There are abbreviations, codes and new words popping up all the time in the ever-evolving world of technology. It can be hard to keep up to speed if it's not our industry. And it is shocking to discover that in the financial sector, language is often used to deliberately confuse people.

Spiritual, 'new age' language can be off-putting to some who prefer a more grounded or practical example or explanation of what can often be the same concept. You may be familiar with some of these terms: manifestation, law of attraction, receiving downloads, spiritual detoxing, holding space, being in resonance, goddess, balancing the masculine and feminine, shamanism, tantra, energy vortexes, consciousness, high vibrations, being authentic and abundance manifestation. (I've used a lot of them in this book!).

There's a fantastic and very amusing video on YouTube called, *Shit New Age Girls Say*[42] that went viral some years ago now with over a million views. In this series of comic videos, the actors parody what groups of guys and girls say within different cultures and races such as the 'New Age' language used by people today. It's so spot on and very interesting to witness the specific languages that have been cultivated by these groups that those 'outside' of the group or bubble may not understand.

THE METAPHYSICAL CLOUD

Humans all have access to the same universal pools of information. These pools of information are like a metaphysical cloud. The information that we 'download' from this cloud is interpreted in many different ways by everyone in their various bubbles. We all tap into these pools, be that consciously or subconsciously and then focus the information through our 'purpose'. That is, in a way that feels good and in a way that uses our natural gifts and talents; just like I'm doing right now in writing this book. The information in this book probably already exists in another form or a book written by someone else in their own unique language. Yet no one else can write a book in the way that I have written this one. My unique life experiences are my fodder; they are what inform the way I write and how I construct and communicate what I want. I 'download' information from the 'cloud' and channel it into my unique expression. And yet we are not

---

[42] Watch 'Shit New Age Girls Say' here: http://youtu.be/iOavbyDKSi0.

just mere 'channels' of an external source of information. **We are active co-creators and artists in unison with the universe.**

The same message reaches more people by using different 'languages' to communicate it. It appeals to different genres and groups in society. The essence or core of the message usually stays intact regardless of what language is used to express it. You may begin to see the connections, the golden threads of truth between all of these 'languages' and different forms of expression in different bubbles.

EXCLUSIVITY IN BUBBLES

We're all drawn to go to specific workshops or read books or watch movies or go to certain cafes because the energy of that 'thing' hits an emotional chord inside us. It might be joy, familiarity, excitement, wonder or curiosity. We like the feeling of it, the words that are used to describe them, the colours or graphics used in the advert or we are interested in the person who has written the book or who is leading the workshop. We are drawn in by the way it makes us feel, our desire to expand and the belief that our needs will be met or that we may feel uplifted or receive guidance to move us forward on our journeys.

I once met a spiritual teacher who used a very unusual language to talk, write and present his work. I found myself getting irritated, as I didn't get why he would purposefully create a bizarre new age language that would exclude a lot of people who might otherwise benefit from what he had to teach, if it were communicated in a language more people could understand. He explained that he only wanted to work with people of a certain level of conscious awareness, people that had been on their spiritual journey for a long time. He *created exclusivity through his use of language, so that only a small, yet defined group of people would be drawn to the courses and workshops he offered, because that is what he wanted. He knew who his 'tribe' was and what language they spoke. That is called focused marketing!*

Often within fields such as spirituality or writing, people *intentionally* use very bizarre, complex or specialised languages. There is a place for exclusivity, if you only want to work with certain groups of people. So individualised language can actually be a very good thing. From a marketing perspective, it's essential to be authentic in our use of language as it allows us to work with the kinds of people we want to work with and to find our 'tribe'. Individually we use a vast variety of 'languages' to communicate similar messages, therefore, we have a much wider outreach because of their differences. Because of this, we can touch and change the lives of many more people from all walks of life.

The *Purpose* Pleasure Project

1. What were your favourite things to do as a child and who did you dream of 'being'?

2. What 'bubbles' do you thrive being in? (Sailing club, psychology, IT, mompreneurs, yoga world, foodie groups, etc).

3. You can create YOU the way you want to be and not the way you think you are; so, who is the YOU in relation to your purpose, that you've always seen yourself being, but are perhaps not currently living?

- What do you look like? What are you wearing and how do you feel wearing it?
- What do you feel like when you are doing and living your purpose?
- What are you doing?
- Who are you doing it with?
- How would you fill your days?

4. What do you value in life? What is important to you to be and to do?

5. If money were no issue, how would you like to contribute and make a difference in the world?

6. At the end of your life, how do you want people to remember you and what would you have liked to have experienced or 'achieved'?

Chapter Summary

- You are a unique and intricate map of the sum of many things. No one has ever existed that is like you and no one ever will
- Bring the energy and essence of you into your practical expressions
- Become aware of the 'bubbles' that you live in and remember to move around in them!
- Return to your childhood joys and passions to bring momentum into your purpose

CHAPTER THIRTEEN

The Language of Freedom

Freedom is flow, it is surfing the feminine love-longing, like a bird surfs an air current, feeling the motion, playing with the poetry of the elements, alive on the life ride and swiftly changing direction when the wind says west.

Freedom is to touch the foundations of the holy temple of your infinite and divine nature. It is to know who you are beneath the name, the dress, the word and the work. It is to find your delicate dance with life, your place in the universe claimed with a bold 'I am' and your stake firmly planted with the flag of your eternal being billowing in the air flow.

Freedom is flow *and* foundation. Your freedom can be found echoing in deep, red canyons or lining the walls of your living room. It is yours to claim, to be or to give away as you wish.

FREEDOM DESIRE

The desire for freedom moves deep. Freedom to express, to speak, to move, to love, to live dreams, fulfil visions or to follow an internal impulse. Free in nature, when we moved in tribes, when we *belonged*. In belonging, we can also find freedom.

In fact, we can feel freedom in any situation, because feeling free is a state of *being* not *doing*. Being free doesn't have a particular look to it, other than the radiance and open energy of the free individual; the person who knows that they are always free.

Simply *knowing* we are free creates an expansive feeling in our individual universe.

We don't need to have freedom *from* something or someone in order to be free. Freedom is not to be had, it just is. Your definition of what freedom is, may actually be limiting your sense of freedom. When someone feels stuck, they wish to feel free from their inner constriction. Perhaps from the confines of daily life and from their responsibilities, yet it's possible to feel great freedom in those responsibilities. Responsibility can actually help us to feel free when we find meaning in the commitments and agreements we make with each other. Living meaningful lives blossoms our sense of fulfilment and freedom. Equally, structure can also provide a sense of freedom for some, as structure offers a clear and solid foundation in which there is room to move. From our own skeletal structures, to the structures within our DNA and all of nature, to our government, business and education models; in as much as the latter are far from 'perfect', they still provide structures we can move and feel supported within and can be a launching platform to freedom.

Freedom is choice. It is the knowing that we can tap into a field of infinite potential and choose something else at any time. And not just that we can choose to change our outside circumstances, like our job or home, but that we can choose to *feel* differently and to change our perspective.

Just having that knowing can make you feel freedom within, even if you have no intention of changing your life circumstances, you understand that you can. You are not 'locked in' to life as it is.

FREEDOM IN SIMPLICITY

The feeling of a lack of freedom can emerge when we feel overwhelmed and there's just too much going on in life. When we overcomplicate things, there appears to be a lack of spaciousness, because our 'space' is filled with too many details.

Never before have we had so much freedom to choose what kind of lifestyle we want to live. Yet this can bring its own problems. With so much choice, it can be overwhelming and difficult to choose a path and thus, not choose any at all.

The challenge in this society is to keep things simple. More often than not, people are busy doing things. There are always things to do. If we're not working, there are projects to plan, administration to attend to, cleaning to do, social events to organise, gifts to buy, travel arrangements to be made, time to be spent in nature, to exercise, regular grocery shopping, even our downtime can be filled with doing (social media anyone!?). When going on dates or making love gets added to the 'things to do list', then forget about sensual surrender. We can all get so caught up in our need to do and to finish the housekeeping tasks that it can be easy to lose sight of our freedom. Especially the freedom that can be found in the simple things.

Profound creations and experiences, like a touching poem or a song or a deep sense of connection and love whilst sitting beneath a tree, are also the most simple. There may be many hidden layers and depth, a poem may even seem bottomless in its meaning and mystery and yet it is simple. Each word is like a hand-picked diamond, plucked and carved from cavernous caves; clean and clear in expression. Many truly inspired moments happen quickly. The product of these inspired moments, through their simplicity, become so popular because the mind doesn't have time to get over-involved, to over-analyse, pick to pieces and basically ruin a simple, creative and clean creation, such as a piece of music.

But why does simple often equal profound? What is it about simple books, songs, articles, poems, movies, living spaces, experiences and even holidays that make them feel so good? Why is the phrase 'Less is more' so famous?

Within something simple, there is room to expand and to stretch. There is spaciousness within the creation that feels freeing and we can feel space in which to breathe. There is movement within the creation. Just as if you were dancing in a large empty space, you can feel your movement. You can feel the freedom and expression of your body so much more than if the room were packed wall to wall with people. You get to feel yourself in the same way within a simple creation and see how it applies itself *to* you and to your life. The simplicity of the words of a poem, song or book expresses the essence of it. Essence is quality, it is concentrate, it is the acorn from which the grand oak tree sprouts and grows. That essence, that quality, the naturalness and simplicity therein *is* the profundity that touches our hearts and souls.

FREEDOM IN CREATIVE EXPRESSION

Through singing, dancing, acting or writing we can take on different roles and allow other aspects of our character to emerge. We get to 'be' and express many other aspects which we might not allow ourselves to express in our usual daily interactions. One of the reasons we can feel such joy when we dance with abandon to music, paint, act in a play or write, is because we feel freedom within, whether we feel restricted by our outside life circumstances or not. That feeling of freedom is expansive and it opens our hearts. We express more of who we really are and that feels good.

INTEGRATION TIME

If you are someone that takes time to process experiences and to integrate them into your being and your life, then taking on too much can seem incredibly overwhelming. Many people often have delayed reactions to situations and experiences. It could be an argument or heated discussion, a tender moment, a big or small decision. Often, it's not until the experience has passed that the 'ah-ha' moment arrives.

If you over-stimulate and overwhelm yourself with too much information, then you create a build-up of experiences and knowledge from last week and the week before that you still haven't given time to integrate into your being. It's like finishing a fantastic novel that leaves you in awe and wonder and as you're closing the last page, you pick up another story by a different author and begin to read straight away. The previous story in the novel you just finished doesn't get a chance to develop, integrate or settle before you're occupied and swept into the next story.

More often than not, many of us don't understand the full significance of an experience until after it has happened, even if we were fully present in that moment. Further insights and connections can continue to come for years after an experience. The clarity of the lessons we learn from many similar experiences can have an accumulative effect, often called an 'enlightened' or a 'eureka' moment, where the sum of all our experiences suddenly makes perfect sense. When we stop and be still to reflect for some time, we allow the integration of experiences and our learning from them to happen. The next phase of life can then begin from a place of clarity, with a greater sense of freedom, acceptance and gratitude within.

THE FREEDOM OF TRAVEL

SHE TRAVELS

She travels,
like the wind
she said,
light and flickering
sashaying
skin to skin.

Or blustering
nipping,
diving,
every which where.

Sometimes she travels
like a hurricane
shaking bodies up,
leaving debris
in her wake.

Her cool breeze
dries sweat-
drivelled faces
travelling heavy.

She travels,
like the wind
she says,

light and blustering,

cooling,

skin to skin.[43]

—*Jane Alexandra Cormack*

For many, freedom can be found in travel. To go where and when we please. To follow an inner calling, as and when it spontaneously arises. Freedom is listening to that calling and moving on it. But the restrictions we place upon ourselves in life often hinder our movement. We block out the calling because of statements or beliefs such as, 'there's not enough money', or 'I've got a house, a family, a job here to do, I can't listen to this calling; I must suppress it and push it inward'. I'm not suggesting that you quit your job, split up from your partner or abandon your children on a whim; that would not be healthy. Whims and deep callings are very different.

We are ultimately free to following our inner calling. Doing so may cause major upheaval, the breakup of relationships, even the selling of all that we own; or no such dramatic changes at all. But know that the choice is there.

Following these callings often lead to the greatest adventures and most profound moments in life as we explore different cultures, their spirituality, food, creativity, customs and natural landscapes.

When I was twenty, my best friend and I set off on our first duo adventure and travelled by rail throughout Europe for six weeks, just following our instincts and the Language of the World as I know it now, as to where to go next. Then, at twenty-one, I wanted to venture out on my own and spent a month travelling through France and Spain. I felt the freedom of being open to the flow of energy and where my intuition guided me to go.

---

[43] Jane Alexandra Cormack, 2009.

Initially, I planned to spend all my time in France and the small island of Corsica, but having no definite plans meant I could choose a new potential in the moment, which I did. I ended up having a fantastic time in Barcelona, Spain, instead!

So much of my 'training' to listen and communicate with the Language of the World was amplified with crystal clarity on my travels or living abroad. The world is my home and my teacher and I can feel at home wherever I feel called to be. When I travel, if possible, I like to spend long periods of time getting to know a place and to connect with the local people and the culture. During my stay I synchronistically meet people who guide me to potent, magical places and experiences. I hear a word or have a feeling and follow it. I feel the spark behind me and instinctively move. This guidance from the universe mirrors my internal universe and may lead me to a new person who carries a message to share or a new place or a country where I should live and be part of the community. **The keys are: Trust - Feel – Listen – Move.**

SHE TRAVELS

At 22, I began planning my first big international trip to North and South America, which was to last five months. I had just graduated from Art School and decided that after visiting Boston and then friends in Phoenix, Arizona, I would fly to Peru and then probably travel through Bolivia. From there I didn't have a clue where to go. I sat in my brightly painted flat in Aberdeen, Scotland, contemplating. I felt the urge to go out for a walk around the streets where I lived at the time. After strolling through several streets of large, granite houses, I came full circle, on my way back to my flat. My attention was brought to an empty glass bottle that lay on the pavement. I kicked it. It rolled over and on the label of the bottle it said, 'Foz De Iguaçu, Brazil'; there was a picture of a majestic waterfall underneath. I felt a flutter of excitement in my belly on seeing the label and was inspired to go home to check on Google what Foz De Iguaçu was. I discovered that Foz De Iguaçu is a city in Brazil, home to world famous waterfalls that span both Brazil and Argentina and that can also be seen from Paraguay. I felt even more excited when I saw the images online of stunning, cascading waterfalls filled with rainbows and surrounded by lush, tropical flora and fauna. In that moment, I decided I would go there. I listened. After travelling through North America, then Peru, Bolivia and Paraguay, I went to Foz De Iguaçu with a friend that I had met on my travels in Peru. As we stood in the jungle, near the water's edge, thousands of giant butterflies fluttered around us and landed on my head and hands, rainbows shone through the water mist created by the falls and a cheeky monkey stole my friend's ice-cream. We took a speed boat up the magnificent Iguaçu River, underneath the falls I felt exhilarated by the power and energy of the water. It was awe inspiring to be so close to such incredible ferocity and breathtaking beauty. Needless to say, it was spectacular and an unforgettable adventure and I was led there by listening to the Language of the World.

My travels around the world have been rich in synchronicity, creativity and heart connection with all the joys and challenges that also come from regularly moving from place to place. These journeys have been intuitive callings from within me. I might say that I followed my heart, my bliss or divine guidance; what I really followed was a *feeling* that felt joyful, exciting and expansive, which led to some of the most potent and enriching experiences of my life.

Travelling is a way for us to stay curious about life and to create connections with new people and cultures that also fulfils our sense of adventure. However, travel, need not be to exotic or far-flung places. A trip to a local garden, or even an afternoon spent walking around your neighbourhood can bring spaciousness and surprising adventures which can lead to inner discoveries and guidance, revealing that the Language of the World is present at all times, in all places. Our world is such a gracious teacher and through travel, near or far, we can discover ourselves and reclaim the magic and language of life.

The *Freedom* Pleasure Project

1. **During which moments have you felt the most freedom in your life?**

- What were you doing?
- Who were you with?
- What aspects of yourself were you being?
- How did you feel?

2. **What does being free mean to you?**

3. **Which forms of creative expression help you to feel free and expand your sense of self?**

Try exploring this feeling by being creative now. Use your Pleasure Project journal to write on freedom, or dance it out in front of a video camera focusing on freedom, act your freedom by trying on different 'roles' or 'characters', paint it on huge pieces of paper or create a collage of images that ignite your freedom desires.

4. **What responsibilities do you have that also make you feel free because they are meaningful to you?**

5. **Design your free life: What are you currently choosing in your life that feels heavy and draining to you?**

6. **What would you now like to choose instead that feels freeing and expansive to you?**

Try creating more spaciousness and simplicity in your environment and your schedule and notice if you feel a wider sense of freedom because of this.

Or perhaps you have too much space in your life? It may be that you require a stronger sense of 'holding' with more structure or a solid foundation to feel a wider or deeper sense of freedom. What do you need to feel free?

Chapter Summary

- Freedom is a state of being
- There is great freedom in simplicity
- You can find freedom in your creativity to explore other aspects of who you are
- Your meaningful responsibilities can also help you to feel free
- Take time to integrate your experiences and create space for freedom and release
- Travel can ignite your freedom desire

CHAPTER FOURTEEN

The Language of Nature

There is a rising desire within the hearts of the modern, creative spiritual woman. It is the desire for deeper fulfilment, freedom, pleasure, meaningful connection, truth and authenticity. Yes, most of us want to stay connected to the modern world, to enjoy business success, stay technologically aware and utilise this for our financial freedom. And many of us love to be inspired by creative fashion and beauty, to luxuriate, to enjoy cafe culture and city living. Yet, this is not enough; an even deeper calling arises from within the soul.

As the awakening of the divine feminine grows within us individually and collectively, you may also feel the instinctual 'pull' to free the wilder parts of you and reconnect with nature and the Earth. But, perhaps the visual image of hairy hippies or crazy and wild-looking witchy women living in the woods may have held you, and many other smart, modern, creative and spiritual women back from accepting and showing your wild and primal elements in public, for fear of being labelled a bit weird or woo-woo?

This pull is an instinctual calling within to return to the origins of who we are as humans on this beautiful planet. The longing that is growing within so many of us is to connect to these primal roots, to the raw and pure energy of nature, to the wild; to the native spirit in us all that's so in tune with life, nature and each other that we know when the rain is coming because we can smell it in the air. **We know when the moon will**

be full without looking it up on Google because our bodies and lives are in tune with the rhythms of the natural world. You may long to feel part of a 'tribe', to be heart-connected, to feel free and open, to be who you authentically are and have your feet connected to the earth. You may have a growing desire to live from the land, to return to your origins, your body and your joy, while still living in love with your laptop, connecting you with your global family.

As we have evolved, we have brought together two worlds that have previously been seen separately; nature and technology. And it's important to cultivate a connection to both.

This longing to connect with nature and our primal roots grows stronger in many women as they enter into the menstrual phase of their cycles and feel a need and desire to be closer to the Earth. Now is an especially good time to acknowledge and embrace the primal and wilder aspects of our nature. This reflects the female body's connection to Earth and nature, as discussed in chapter 4, Feminine Power.

THE FREQUENCY OF NATURE

I love to begin the day in nature, to go outside and greet the world. Welcoming a new day with gratitude in my garden or a local nature spot usually sets me up in a positive state of body and mind for the day. When we are in a place where there is no Wifi, radio, mobile or technology waves of any kind (harder to find these places now!) then it becomes easier to feel the similar waves of energy that emit from nature. The universe is filled with vibrational frequencies that we can tune-in to. It becomes possible to *hear* these 'waves' through *feeling* them. We can tune-in to the frequency of nature just as we tune-in to the different channels on a radio to find a station we want to listen to.

This process of tuning-in can be applied to everything, including other people and animals.

HOW NATURE CULTIVATES CLARITY

Clarity often comes when we tune-in to nature because we are connecting to a pure frequency. An ancient, raw and real energy that is the foundation of life on Earth. Nature contains 'source'[44] energy just as we do and so when we tune-in to nature's source, then we are connecting to the very essence of life that also lives within us. It feels like coming home. We are reminded of our primal origins. When we connect at this level, all the things we may have been worrying about can melt away. We get closer to the essence of who we truly are. And when we experience who we truly are, we are clearer about what we really want and are an open channel for inspiration to flow through.

In 2005, I lived in Australia and had decided to go on a road trip from Sydney to Brisbane to visit a friend. After spending some time in Brisbane, we did some travelling together back down south meandering our way in and out the coast. My friend wanted to show me the Dorrigo rainforest, so we travelled through the small town of Bellingen and stopped by Dorrigo National Park. As we stood on the wooden deck overlooking this ancient forest, a well of emotion surged through me. Mid-conversation with my friend, I began to cry. It was an incredible feeling of heart-opening release. The raw and ancient energy of this magical rainforest ignited in me the memory of my origins. It returned me to the 'knowing' of who

---

[44] When I refer to 'Source', I refer to what you may know as life-force energy, divinity or God.

I really am on the deepest level. I stood there on the deck over-looking the forest and cried for a long time, unable to find words to describe how I felt. The memories that were released were the memories in my DNA, my ancestral heritage and the connection to our ancient and primal human lineage as well as to the Earth before humans even existed upon it.

Dorrigo rainforest has existed for millions of years on this planet. It's part of the Gondwara Rainforests of Australia World Heritage Area which is, "The most extensive strip of diverse rainforest anywhere on Earth".[45] The forest is, "A link to the ancient, pre-human world"[46], which for me was an energetic link that unlocked cellular memories of my origins on the planet. Just as we entrain to other people, as discussed in chapter 5, Love and Relationships, we also entrain to our environments. To have such records of life on this planet is incredibly precious and so very powerful to help activate the ancient memories that lie within us all.

Our gradual disconnection from nature and living in tribes mirrors the disconnection so many people are feeling from themselves, their 'tribes' and the planet. When we are disconnected in this way, it's easy to forget what truly matters, who we really are, and to trust in life. Yet, this sense of inner knowing is always present, although often ignored as we go about our continual daily doings that we can't seem to stop doing and give great importance to.

When we connect to the source within ourselves, we also simultaneously connect to the source within all things, within life itself. So if you make connecting to your inner source a daily practice then the more grounded, 'in' your power and alive you feel and become. Like a forest of

---

[45] http://www.nationalparks.nsw.gov.au/Dorrigo-National-Park

[46] As above.

bamboo, you are firmly planted in the earth, rooted there with the support of earth and yet you are also flexible, versatile and moveable. From your foundations, you can bend and stretch, swaying in the wind, in rhythm with all the other bamboo in the forest around you.

THE ESSENCE OF NATURE

Each tree, plant, flower, mineral and metal on our planet has a specific and different energy. Trees, plants, birds, animals, water, sun, moon, stars, mountains, their colours and scents and all of nature have a voice and speak to us. Each species conveys a different message through its essence which you can learn to feel. Their language is expressed simply by their *being* what they are. A peach rose emits its beautiful scent, its colour glows and its petals are soft, velvety and intricately detailed. Your personal association of what a peach rose feels like and what it may remind you of will be different to someone else's association, but most people can see and sense the essential beauty of the rose.

THE ROSE AND THE DAISY

Take the peach rose and look at it side by side with a wild, garden daisy. A peach rose has many layers, its petals softly curved, velvety to touch, curving inwards to protect the centre. The oil from a rose is considered valuable, it's one of the most precious and expensive essential oils on the planet. It takes around five thousand pounds of fresh rose petals to make just one pound of essential oil. Rose oil has many healing properties including nourishing dry skin by helping to soften fine lines. It is an aphrodisiac and antiseptic, it's antiviral, an anti-depressant and great for soothing stress and nervousness as well as for poor circulation. Rose oil also helps to stimulate hormonal secretion in the body generating menstruation in women. Its scent is sweet and is used in perfumes; it is voluptuous in appearance, sensual and mysterious, beautiful, soft and inviting, it is associated with femininity. It also has razor sharp thorns on its long, strong stem that can slice fingers open. It is seductive, beautiful and dangerous; the dark and the light both serve their purpose, creating the whole. Within the family of roses there are hundreds of varieties. From Christmas roses to miniature or wild roses in all colours, shapes, sizes and scents. The rose is much admired and prized, gloriously symbolising a feminine flower.

A wild garden daisy is much smaller in stature to the common peach rose. It has a fragile, thin stem and grows much closer to the earth. Its shape is fairly uniform with white, straight petals that are open revealing the bright yellow, fuzzy centre. Daisies can be found sprinkled widely and sporadically over grass and meadows. Daisies are dainty and pretty and have no identifiable scent. Its colours are simple and clean. The daisy contains medicinal properties that soothe sore muscles and wounds and is a natural remedy for M.E.[47] Within the family of daisies there are large and small and a variety of often vibrant, bright colours. Can you sense the difference between the feeling of the daisy in comparison to the rose?

The same example can be made between any plant, flower or tree. Even by observing the look, feel and natural habitat of different trees and plants, we can begin to tune-in to the distinct energy of each flower or tree. We can experience its essence and receive what it gives simply by it *being* what it is. Nature does not hide from humans. Humans often just choose not to see what is already there.

If you can see that nature teaches you by 'being' what it is, then **you may see how simple it is to 'be' a great teacher yourself, simply by**

---

[47] Myalgic Encephalomyelitis also known as Chronic Fatigue Syndrome (C.F.S).

virtue of being who you already are. We are all the same species, just as all flowers are flowers and yet we all have an individual look, sound and energy. Our own essence is expressed in many ways. Our race, colour, height, shape, voice, accent, language, smell and movement are all ways through which our unique essence is expressed, as discussed in chapter 12, Purpose. We are as individual as a rose or a daisy and yet we are all from the same family.

There is beauty in our 'being' when we allow ourselves the freedom to be who we are and to fully accept ourselves. It can take encouragement to open our hearts and show the world all our beauty, our light and shadows, because it can feel frightening. When we can much more deeply and openly appreciate and celebrate our differences, we learn that we are all different for many good reasons. We each have something valuable to contribute in our own wonderful ways to the greater good of humanity, and the growing consciousness of the planet.

INFUSING NATURE ENERGY THROUGH YOUR CREATIVE EXPRESSION

Nature has its own music, its own colours and textures, it is its own poetry and sings its own song in its own rhythm. The canvas of nature feeds our spirit and activates our senses, flowing life-force fuel through our veins. Throughout history, the energy of nature has inspired human creativity, in various art forms.

Nature is our food and our medicine, it is our home. It provides both the foundation for our life on the planet and an infinite source of inspiration, mystery and wonder. Our natural world is a place to explore and is an awe-inspiring adventure. It is our source of great joy and pleasure and should be revered, respected and touched with loving hands.

In each place we travel to and visit, we can connect to nature in that country. We can be inspired by its unique energy and create unique art. In this way, we co-create with nature, through our own creative expression.

I was incredibly excited to watch Icelandic music icon Björk alongside legendary naturalist and broadcaster Sir David Attenborough in the 2013 documentary, 'When Björk met Attenborough'.[48] Björk was born and grew up in Iceland, a country where there is so much untouched land held beneath acres of ice, still intact after millions of years. The 'primitive' and ancient energy is very strong because of this—it's a raw energy that can be heard and sensed in Björk's music.

In this documentary interview, Björk talks about her multi-media project, 'Biophilia' and shares the great influence of nature in her music and creations. She expresses how she harnessed the visual power of music on stage, by combining the science of nature with the science of music and technology so that we can 'see' music as well as hear it. Her influences include the structure of mineral crystals from the earth, layers of rock, lightening and animal and plant structures. Björk has created apps that use our intuitive understanding of the natural world, to create music, for example, what lightening can teach about *arpeggios*, the musical notes that are played or sung in sequence. These apps are now a standard part of the educational music curriculum in Iceland.

Regardless of where we are, there is the ever-present universal Language of the World. Through the natural environment, we can hear this communication in its purest form and infuse this energy into everything that we create.

[48] *When Björk met Attenborough*, Dir. Louise Hooper, Producer, Caroline Page, (UK, 2013, Channel 4). http://www.channel4.com/programmes/when-bjork-met-attenborough/on-demand.

THE LANGUAGE OF NATURE

"She had a powerful feeling that she was part of this living organism. That they even shared the same heart. She recognised this energy of the Earth as her own and felt the energy of the group move into the core of the world. There was a feeling of equality, of the Earth as theirs, but that they belonged to the Earth".[49]

We are born with this connection to Earth, but often grow more distant from it as we become 'socialised' into our modern lives. Yet, the sense of our original connection always remains somewhere beneath the surface, often calling us back at certain times in our lives to reclaim it. Nature is a powerful teacher and messenger and we need only observe more closely to see and feel what nature communicates with us every moment. Sometimes, it can be as simple as taking a walk in your local wooded copse and sitting beneath a tree for a while. Breathe and be present to see and feel what's around you and be open to what comes to you in those moments. Perhaps it may be a feeling of deep peace or new ideas, thoughts, insights or messages. In these moments you are talking, you are speaking the Language of the World.

The language of nature contains all of the Languages of the World. It is expressed through its scent, colour, texture, essence, heat, through symbol and the music of nature. Nature is our home and sanctuary space where we can feel free and sense the clarity of our purpose.

Do you have a clearer picture of how you already know the Language of the World now and how to experience the language of the feminine?

You have been communicating all of your life. We *all* have. Through learning to listen and feel more deeply to read the signs, you can enjoy your conversations with the universe in new ways.

---

[49] Excerpt from short story by Jane Cormack.

Receiving simple messages from the Language of the World via nature can arrive in unusual ways...

HOW DOES YOUR GARDEN GROW?

I began making weekly video blogs, sharing tips, tools and practices to inspire, connect and raise consciousness through creativity in early 2012. My video, 'How Does Your Garden Grow? ~ Celebrating Our Creative Progress,' was filmed in a polytunnel in the Spiritual and Eco Community of Findhorn, in Northeast Scotland. I likened our own personal growth and the growth of humanity to the way nature grows; steadily and in spurts. That day, I returned to my new flat which was still being gradually furnished by the owner. She had put a new mug in the cupboard. On it were the words, 'A Garden Is Never Finished'. I smiled to myself because this was a very clear message from the universe, especially after the video I had just created, that no matter how much we grow, we never stop growing.

There is no end result, no finale in which we find our growth has ended and that the garden of our personal and spiritual growth is finally complete. We continue our growth and no matter how long we live on this planet, there are always new things to experience.

The *Nature* Pleasure Project

In this project, you'll learn how to begin a conversation with nature beginning simply with focus and observation.

1. Gather your Pleasure Project journal and a pen and either find a place in nature to settle, or if the weather isn't appealing, get comfy in your home and find a house plant to focus on. If you are outside, you might choose a blade of grass, a flower, a leaf, a tree or a whole mountain.

2. Give ALL of your attention to the nature object of your focus. Look deep into its essence, see the minute detail, the veins in the leaf, the colours and textures and then look at the whole. Breathe its essence into you until you feel filled and connected to your nature object. Can you feel the essence of it? This is its voice and its message through being what it is.

3. Now, begin to write in your journal any words that you may find emerging from this connection. Just allow them to come out as they are, you're not trying to be Hafiz or Rumi so just let go and begin with what you see. Then you can move onto your other senses, what you feel and what you hear in connection with your piece of nature.

Follow the link in the footnote[50] to watch my YouTube video 'How to Meditate with Creative Expression', to be led through the process of meditating on an aspect of nature and expressing this connection through poetry.

HOW WE CAN REGENERATE AND REPLENISH OUR ENERGY

There is an unlimited source of energy from which we can regenerate.

To give from a place of fullness, we can regenerate from the universal source of energy found in all of the natural world and its elements:

- Nature
- Earth
- Sun
- Pure water
- Breath/air

[50] Cormack, Jane, How to Meditate with Creative Expression: http://www.janecormack.com/rhythmic-inspiration-news/how-to-meditate-with-creative-expression/.
On YouTube: http://www.youtube.com/watch?v=Y3828NY5lkQ.

We can replenish and come back to balance within through:

- Stillness and quiet time
- Inward focus
- Body cleanse
- Unplugging from all technology for a while
- Spending time alone in nature walking or meditating
- Doing something that you know makes you feel joyful
- Creating a Pleasure Project to focus on what does give you pleasure

Tune-in to the kind of nature environment you feel drawn to go to on different days. Near water, an ocean, river, stream or lake? In the mountains at high altitude? In a tall forest of pine trees? A jungle, your local park or a sandy beach; what calls to you now?

Notice how these different environments inspire you and then infuse the energy of nature into your creative expression.

▌ Chapter Summary

- When you awaken to your divine feminine nature within, you may feel magnetically 'pulled' to connect more deeply with nature—listen to that
- Nature contains and emits a frequency
- You can infuse the energy of nature into everything that you create
- Nature is a language, it can be considered THE Language of the World
- Nature supports us to get clear and reminds us who we are at core level

CHAPTER FIFTEEN

The Language of the World and Your Pleasure

Language surrounds us. It is us. It is spoken by the wind, the music in your ear, it is the love in your heart. Your world and reality are like the shifting sands of time in the desert and the language that you hear guides your direction. Language fills us, it is everything and everywhere. It's the last sentence spoken on a TV show that catches your imagination, the mentioning of a book overheard in conversation standing at the train station. It is the gleeful laughter of a baby in her pram lifting and lightening your heart, it's the scent of freshly ground coffee leading you to the corner cafe and new friends. It is your own knowing, it is your vision, it is nature calling you home, it is you. It is the language of life and the feminine.

The universe moves with us and within us. We *are* the universe, and the universe *is* us. Our Earth is a moving, evolving, pulsating organism and we are guided by her rhythms. When we reclaim the feminine element, we listen to and follow those rhythms, we experience our connection with the Earth, and the magical and often mysterious unfolding of life. The world needs this element, it needs the infusion of our feminine in the way we care and love, in the way we treat and live in the environment, in our educational and government systems and the way we connect and communicate with each other, both professionally and personally.

Reclaiming our feminine element can begin in joy, as we awaken to the source of our creative, intuitive and sensual self and begin to own and trust in the immense power, magic and wisdom that we all possess.

It can be easy to forget to deliberately and regularly do things that feel joyful and instead spend most of our time doing what we think we 'should' be doing. We all need regular reminders to return to love, pleasure and joy. In doing so, we offer an environment for the Language of the Feminine to flourish.

The *joy* Pleasure Project

Think about five things, experiences and people that give you JOY!
Five experiences I love to do and that make me feel really joyful and happy are:

1.

2.

3.

4.

5.

Five people that inspire, encourage, love me and make me feel good to be around are:

1.

2.

3.

4.

5.

Five things I love to look at, use or create (like art, books, colour etc) are:

1.

2.

3.

4.

5.

Begin today to do, be and surround yourself with the people and things that enhance your joy!

Now check-in with how you feel after doing this exercise.

The *Language of the World* Pleasure Project

1. In the last week alone, recount the ways in which you feel you received or were in communication with the Language of the World:

2. Write down the synchronistic moments that stand out most in your life:

3. Choose three that feel the most prominent and write how you were feeling and what led you to those moments:

4. What symbols, sensations, words, messengers, colours, music, intuitive feeling or something else, showed up as guidance?

5. Write a list of all the things you love in this world; it may be figuring out equations, playing the sitar, going to the gym, enjoying the drive from your house to visit your auntie, watching your child open birthday presents, making clocks, sitting on mountain tops, making love to your partner, lying in a meadow watching cloud formations float by; there are so many things to love in life. What do you love? Write between ten to fifteen things that you love here:

1)

2)

3)

4)

5)

6)

7)

8)

9)

10)

Continue in your Pleasure Project journal until you feel complete.

6. After writing a list of what you love, write what you feel whilst you are doing the top five things from the list that you love:

   1)

   2)

   3)

   4)

   5)

7. Now, write how often you do those things: Daily? Once or twice a week? Once a month, once a year or every few years?

8. How often would you like to do them?

9. In what ways, through the things you love, do you see how the Language of the World has been communicating with you?

10. **What do you want to create? Write a list of the forms in which you want to express and communicate your wisdom and knowledge. (It might be a new blog post or video, a children's story, a world tour, a music album, a cake, a book, a conference, a fashion line, a play or a multi-creative empire; don't hold back!):**

11. **What steps will you now take to do and experience more of what you love?**

Feel this connection to what fills you with joy and keep it. It will help to strengthen you and give you confidence and clarity to always feel connected to your own inner source. It will help you to lead from that place and *be* the source.

Bring your awareness back to your body sitting where you sit right now, reading this book. Feel your breath moving through you, in through your nose and down within your body. Breathe in fully and deeply allowing the breath to circulate through your body, enhancing your life-force. Feel the parts of your body that are physically connected to the chair or floor and be present where you sit right now. Open your eyes.

The Language of the World is talking, are you ready to listen?

Acknowledgements

My gratitude goes out to my sanctuary space in Findhorn, Scotland, where this book began finding its form. It was from this supportive environment that I felt held to begin writing.

My thanks go to the Yule family for giving me such a wonderful writing space at 'The Hut'. My love and appreciation go to Alexandra Mahlimay for your experience, wisdom, honesty and love and to Heather 'Hev' Drummond for your support, humour and vast reading experience. I also want to thank and acknowledge the wonderful Eliza Kiers who was impatiently thrown a very early draft of the manuscript and who compassionately read it and returned snippets of boundless enthusiasm. Thank you to Ursula for your encouragement, listening and support and for the nourishment of a cosy sanctuary with cats to cuddle. To Henny, thank you for holding space around the book writing process and appreciations to Alexandra Gold, Patricia Iris Kerins and Yella for sharing your own journey and tips in writing and publishing.

Kefah Bates, my soul sister, I feel so much gratitude for your presence, support and love. Encouragement and 'just do its!' from Sarah Hatcher and Jaime Goode; love you girls! Toni Bate of Indie Publishing, thanks for being my first 'proper' reader, for your positive review and grounding presence. Tanja-Janina Grosse, thank you for reading everything twice so quickly and for your honest and encouraging feedback. Marijke Derese, the joy and enthusiasm you shared after reading the first two chapters spurred me onward, thank you! Aminah Hughes, your poetic mind and heart and your simple, short and clear e-mail made me smile. Kami, Dominique, Nora,

Sabine, Tanja and Nicole, thank you for your intuitive feedback on choosing a great book title.

To Jamie Stewart for re-emerging in my life at the perfect time; thank you for your patience, professionalism, eye for detail and for offering the first male perspective on my writing.

Joan and Matthew Greenblatt, my professional cover and interior designers, thank you for helping to shape my book into a beautiful and readable format.

To my professional author coach, Door De Flines, a truly amazing woman with whom I share a mutual love of books as well as the same birthday; thank you for your incredible support, patience, wisdom, honesty, belief and encouragement and for stretching me beyond my comfort zones. You have played such an integral part in the creation of this book and I'm so grateful for having met you.

I offer two very special thank yous and such deep gratitude to my amazing friends and soul sisters, Marielle van Dop and Katy. Marielle thank you for supporting me in multiple ways, you continue to astound me with your huge and generous heart and love. Thank you for spotting the juice and flow in this text and for your awesome feminine presence and sharp intuition.

Katy, you are my beacon of everlasting friendship, who never fails to light up my world with your wit, joy, cheeky humour, compassionate heart and effervescent life-force. Thank you for your wise, insightful and often hilarious comments on my work. You are a true sister and it fills me with joy to travel through this creative journey of life, knowing that we are a part of each others worlds.

Beautiful A, thank you for listening, for loving, for communicating back to me what you heard, for your patience, presence and depth of sensitivity. You made all the difference.

I feel an unending gratitude and profound love for my family; Mum and Dad you are the most supportive and loving parents anyone could wish for, I am truly blessed, thank you for your support and your love in every way. And to my wonderful brother Ross, for making me laugh, listening and supporting me to get this book 'out there!' Thank you!

I have been inspired by and learnt from many on my path and not just those who are notable teachers, so in mentioning none, I acknowledge all. Profound thanks go to the many mentors, messengers and teachers who have shown up in my life at the perfect time. To all of you who sent encouraging comments or e-mails for me in moments I truly needed them, thank you.

To nature and the clarity that you helped me cultivate and to the Language of the World in all the many forms you spoke to me; to all things seen and unseen showing me a word, a message, a song or a vision, like a trail of breadcrumbs to find, follow and write: I give my thanks.

References

Books & Publications

Northrup, Dr. Christiane, *Women's Bodies, Women's Wisdom—The Complete Guide to Women's Health and Wellbeing* (Piatkus, 1994, 2009, US and Great Britain).

Coelho, Paulo, *The Alchemist*, Harper Collins, 2012 (First English Edition, 1993).

Ladinsky, Daniel/Hafiz, *The Gift, Poems by Hafiz, The Great Sufi Master*, translations by Daniel Ladinsky, Penguin Compass, 1999.

Zeman, Adam; Milton, F.; Smith, A.; Rylance, R, 'By Heart An fMRI Study of Brain Activation by Poetry and Prose'. *Journal of Consciousness Studies, Imprint Academic*, Volume 20, Numbers 9-10, 2013, pp. 132-158(27).

Cameron, Julia, *The Artists Way, A Spiritual Path to Higher Creativity*, Penguin Group (USA), 1992.

von Goethe, Johanne Wolfgang, *Theory of Colours*, translation by Charles Lock Eastgate, John Murray, 1810 (1840 in English).

Groover, Rachael Jayne, *The Art of Feminine Presence Training Manual*, 2012. www.rachaeljayne.com

Cormack, Jane. *Poems of Earth, Heart & Spirit.* Dissertation/Theses, 2009.

Magazines

Cunningham, Emily, 'I've Been to the Quietest Place on Earth', *Guardian Weekend*, 19th May 2012, p17. Online version: www.theguardian.com/ lifeandstyle/2012/may/18/experience-quietest-place-on-earth. George Foy: www.georgefoy.com/index.html

Music

Snow Patrol, 'Run' Rec. February 2003, *Final Straw.* Fiction/Polydor 2004.

Jackson, Michael, 'Man in the Mirror', *Bad.* Rec. February—May 1987. Epic 1988.

Mraz, Jason, 'Back to the Earth'. Rec. 2013- 2014, *Yes!* Atlantic Records, 2014.

Films and Documentaries

In a Small Valley (Deafness in Australia), Dir. Dennis K. Smith, Producer, Jack White (Melbourne, Australia, 1996, Open Channel Productions).

When Björk met Attenborough, Dir. Louise Hooper, Producer, Caroline Page, (UK, 2013, Channel 4). http://www.channel4.com/programmes/when-bjork-met-attenborough

The Butterfly Effect, Dir. Eric Bress, J. MacKye Gruber, (USA, 2004, New Line Cinema).

Pay it Forward. Dir. Mimi Leder (USA, 2000, Warner Brothers Pictures).

Applications

Hay, Louise. L. 'Heal *Your Body A-Z App'.*
http://www.oceanhousemedia.com/products/healyourbody/&legacy/
Oceanhouse Media.

Websites

Lewis, M. Paul, Gary F. Simons and Charles D. Fennig (eds.). 2015. Ethnologue: Languages of the World, Eighteenth edition. Dallas, Texas: SIL International, Online version: www.ethnologue.com

Ethnologue, Languages of the World. *'Endangered Languages':*
www.ethnologue.com/endangered-languages

Dorrigo National Park.
www.nationalparks.nsw.gov.au/Dorrigo-National-Park

Wonderful World of Rose Essential Oil. www.bathpetals.com
(original page on Rose Essential Oil is no longer available). Bath Petals.

Bellis Perenis (Daisy). www.kew.org/plants-fungi/Bellis-perennis.htm.
Kew Royal Botanical Gardens.

Henderson, Cal, 'What is Color Blindness'.
www.iamcal.com/toys/colors/whatis.php. See the colour spectrum of
colour-deficient people here: Henderson, Cal, 'Palettes'.
www.iamcal.com/toys/colors/ (website no longer available, you can view
the work of Cal Henderson at http://network.iamcal.com/).

Quote in Chapter 9, Colour and Creating Yourself used with permission
from Michael Reichmann and sourced from; https://luminous-landscape.
com/colour-theory/

Paul, Annie Murphy. 'Your Brain on Fiction'. http://www.nytimes.
com/2012/03/18/opinion/sunday/the-neuroscience-of-your-brain-on-
fiction.html?_r=0 The New York Times Sunday Review.

Ward, Geoff. 'The Magic of the Spiral'.
www.world-mysteries.com/gw_Geoff_Ward_2.htm. World Mysteries.
Excerpt from: Ward, Geoff, 'Spirals: The Pattern of Existence', Green Magic,
second revised edition, Feb 2013.

Purce, Jill. www.healingvoice.com

Elevate. 'Shit New Age Girls Say'. 13th January 2012. Retrieved from
www.youtube.com/watch?v=iOavbyDKSi0

Cormack, Jane. 'How to Heal the Voice—Interview with Vocal Expert, Jill
Purce'. www.janecormack.com/video-audio/. www.janecormack.com

Cormack, Jane. *'How to Feel Inspired Even When You Feel Flat—On Tour from Mull in Scotland'.* www.janecormack.com/rhythmic-inspiration-news/how-to-be-inspired-even-when-you-feel-flat-on-tour-from-mull-in-scotland/. www.janecormack.com

Cormack, Jane. *'Learn How to Heal the Voice—Special Interview with Vocal Expert, Jill Purce + The Quietest Place on Earth'.* www.janecormack.com/sound-healing/learn-how-to-heal-the-voice-special-interview-with-vocal-expert-jill-purce/. www.janecormack.com

Cormack, Jane. *'How to Meditate with Creative Expression'.* www.janecormack.com/rhythmic-inspiration-news/how-to-meditate-with-creative-expression/. www.janecormack.com

THE END IS JUST THE BEGINNING

About the Author

Jane Cormack, MA, is a writer, designer, artist and certified guide in feminine awakening. She originally founded, 'Rhythm In Colour— Cultivating Courage in Women to Shine', in 2009; a company offering women personal growth events through the multi-creative arts. She has travelled widely and spent time living in Australasia, Continental Europe and the Americas. She is currently based in Europe and facilitates international Feminine Focus circles, workshops, retreats and classes for women to guide them into the awakening of their feminine essence and relationship with their own sense of trust, wisdom, creativity and power.

Discover more at:
www.JaneCormack.com *and* www.LanguageoftheFeminine.com

Share your story! How has the Language of the World
spoken to you and how have you 'been' this language for others?

Connect and Share on:
www.facebook.com/janeAcormack
www.instagram.com/jane.cormack

Notes

Notes